the soccer method

BUILD-UP PLAY

Henk Mariman

Library of Congress
Cataloging - in - Publication Data

the Soccer Method
Book 1 - Build Up Play
by Henk Mariman

ISBN-13: 978-1-59164-103-2
ISBN-10: 1-59164-103-9
Library of Congress Control Number: 2006903026
© 2006

All rights reserved. Except for use in a review.The reproduction or utilization of this book in any form or by any electronic, mechanical or other means, now known or hereafter invented, including xerography, photocopying and recording, and in any information storage and retrieval system, is forbidden without written permission of the publisher.

Editing
Bryan R. Beaver

Translation from Dutch
Dave Brandt

Printed by
Data Reproductions
Auburn, Michigan

Reedswain Publishing
562 Ridge Road
Spring City, PA 19475
www. reedswain.com
info@reedswain.com

Contents

iv   **Introduction**

1   **Work Items**
3   Insight -related aspects
6   Technique-related aspects
7   Goalkeeping-related aspects
8   Aspects of facing 3 or 2 strikers

11   **Tasks and Functions**

15   **The Aims of the Game**
17   The goalkeeper's build up options
25   The defenders' build up options

47   **Coaching Ball Skills**

75   **Coaching Method**
75   Coaching the aims of the game
95   Problem-oriented coaching

111   **Practice Drills**
112   Passing and shooting drills
118   Positional play
124   Line training with 2 lines
132   Line training with 3 lines

Book 1   Build-Up Play

Introduction

Systematic build-up play from the back is not a common feature of youth soccer. Usually the goalkeeper and defenders choose the easiest option and kick the ball upfield. Sometimes purposefully and sometimes just hopefully.

This might prevent the opposition from scoring, but it has its limitations in the long run. Choosing not to encourage systematic build-up play from the back has negative consequences for young players' development.

Build-up play from the back is a key element in the development of young players.

Having more ball contacts and having to make more choices undoubtedly has a favorable influence on the soccer playing ability of a defender.

If a defender expects to receive the ball from his goalkeeper, this will certainly improve his ability to receive and go, and to pass accurately. He will also learn how to receive the ball and turn with it, which is not something that a defender often has to do. This improves his footwork. A defender learns more quickly how to use both feet if he is involved in the build-up play.

This also applies to the goalkeeper. Purposeful build-up play in combination with defenders, midfielders and attackers, and kicking the ball accurately into a given zone or to a specific player help to improve the goalkeeper's all-round skills.

Build-up play from the back is also a crucial aspect of the development of midfielders. If defenders play long balls forward, bypassing the midfielders, the midfielders mainly play a supporting role, facing the opposing team's goal and making forward runs.

A midfielder also needs to be able to receive the ball with his back to his opponent. A midfielder who has only had to run onto passes played back to him as he goes forward will have problems when the ball is played to his feet and he has an opponent behind him. Attackers also benefit from systematic build-up play. Different skills are needed to cope with passes played to feet and passes played into space. Attackers must learn when to make themselves available to receive a pass, and what to do in the follow-up phase.

> "I see youth matches every week. My impression is that pressure is always exerted quickly and the ball is played forward reasonably quickly. There are matches when defenders never seem to pass to midfielders. A central defender does not have to be the most skillful soccer player, but he does have to learn how to play soccer!"
>
> *Ron Spelbos*

Introduction

THE CONTENTS OF THIS BOOK

After reading this book, a coach should be able to incorporate build-up drills in his training sessions. I have divided the build-up module into six sections.

Section 1: All the typical aspects of build-up play that need to be worked on ("work items") are collected here. I have distilled the most important work items from the numerous soccer matches I have watched between teams of young players.

In **section 2**, I define the tasks and functions of the total team, the lines of the team (defense, midfield, attack) and the specific positions (based on a 1-3-4-3 team formation).

In **section 3**, I describe all the aims of build-up play. These aims are aligned to the chosen playing system. There are explanations of the typical aspects that need to be worked on.

Section 4 deals with the ball skills needed during build-up play. These techniques are linked to coaching points and practice drills.

Young soccer players can be coached in 2 ways. The players can learn about the aims of the game, and they can learn about the specific soccer problems revealed by the analysis of real matches. In **section 5**, I explain more about this.

Section 6 contains specific drills. The level of these drills is adapted to the different age groups.

Book 1   Build-Up Play

Section 1 - Work Items

Work Items

Book 1   Build-Up Play

Work items

In recent years I have watched a lot of youth soccer matches at various levels. I have identified the most important aspects of build-up play that need to be worked on and divided them into 5 categories.

- Insight-related aspects
- Technique-related aspects
- Goalkeeping-related aspects
- Aspects of facing a team with 3 strikers
- Aspects of facing a team with 2 strikers

You will recognize some of these items from your own experience. In section 3 (aims of the game), I try to show how to approach them.

Section 1 - Work Items

Insight-related aspects

No build-up play occurs
The players have no intention of building up moves systematically.

Players run with the ball too often
A player who runs with the ball too often is vulnerable and is more likely to lose possession. If a defender runs too far with the ball, he runs the risk of being caught out of position if he loses it, thus opening up options for the opposing team. Moves should be built-up from the back taking as few risks as possible. Players should therefore try to avoid running with the ball when they are in their own half.

> "If you need to keep the ball circulating quickly, one of your players can't just run with the ball. He can't. You can only run with the ball to give a teammate the chance to get into another position."
>
> *Johan Cruijff*

The build-up play is too predictable
If the build-up play always proceeds through the central defender and the defensive midfielder it becomes too predictable. It is important to make choices in relation to the situation. Always making the same choice makes the build-up too vulnerable.

The ball is not played forward into the attacking zones
The defenders and midfielders play the ball to each other but fail to play it forward to the strikers. The play is aimless. The ball is simply played square and back.

The ball is played to the goalkeeper too often
Playing the ball back to the goalkeeper is not always good. It is important for the development of young players that they learn to pass the ball into attacking zones, even if this means that they sometimes lose possession. Getting the ball forward involves a number of skills, such as turning with the ball, first-touch passing, being aware of what is happening, etc. If the ball is played back too often, these skills cannot be developed.

Defenders lack conviction when they run into space
Some players prefer not to have the ball, while others are too casual when they run into space. When a player calls for the ball from the goalkeeper, he must do so with conviction. A sudden acceleration into space is essential in order to shake off a defender.

Players take no risks
If a coach puts too much emphasis on not losing possession, this undermines the players' willingness to show initiative. Young players who take no risks miss out on an important part of their development. The younger the players, the more risks they can take.

The ball is passed down the flank too often
Passing down the wing – e.g. from right back to right winger – is often risky. The opposition can easily defend against this situation.

The build-up is too slow
Getting the ball forward into attacking zones is often a question of speed of execution. While the ball is circulating, there are just a few moments when opportunities arise for passing it into an attacking zone. A lot of soccer has to be played to create a goal-scoring chance. By circulating the ball, a team creates situations in which the opposing team cannot always react sufficiently quickly. These situations provide opportunities for passing the ball into attacking zones. The speed of execution (good communication, high tempo, good ball control, one-touch passes) determines how often such moments occur.

> In adult soccer, a defender who is not comfortable on the ball need not play a decisive part in the build-up play. If this problem arises in youth soccer, the player must be encouraged to develop.

Book 1 — Build-Up Play

There is no communication during the build-up play
Lack of communication is a problem in all youth teams. Coaching keywords can be agreed on to make communication easier.

No message is communicated with the ball
The speed and path of the ball and the direction of the play are not adjusted to suit the situation. In practice, the ball is usually predictably passed to feet. The position of the opponent and the aim of playing the ball into attacking zones are not taken into account.

There is a lack of cooperation in the build-up play
In practice, one of the defenders might call for the ball from the goalkeeper or receive a pass from another player. He is then left to himself. The other players take no action to support him.

There is no space to run into. The players stand too close to the edge of the penalty area.
The players stand too close to the edge of the penalty area or inside it. There is no space for

> How can you expect the players to communicate if you always tell them what to do?

build-up play. Neither defenders nor midfielders are available to receive the ball.

There is enough space for build-up play in and around the penalty area, but the players push forward first before making themselves available again to receive the ball.
An example: The central defender is free and could ask for the ball. Instead, he pushes forward. He then calls for the ball from the goalkeeper.

The build-up players allow themselves to be held back by the opposing striker.
The central defender (3) and the midfielder (4) play the ball back and forth to each other but have no intention of getting past the striker (9). The striker is able to repeatedly block the path of the player in possession.

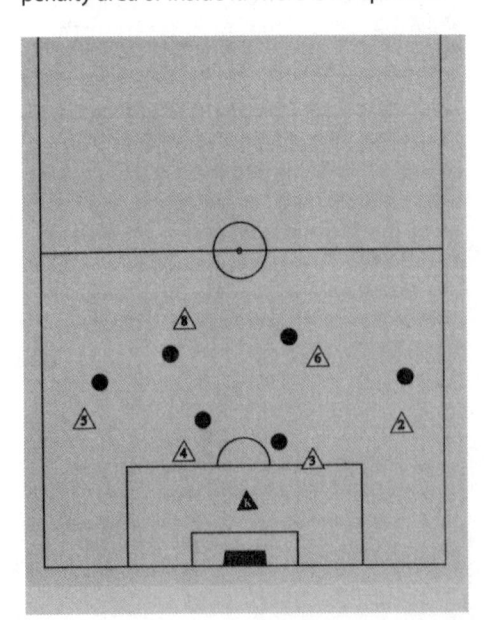

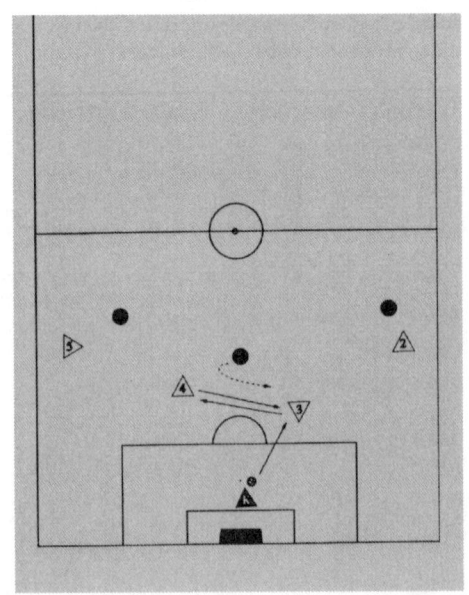

Section 1 - Work Items

The build-up takes place too often down the same side of the field.

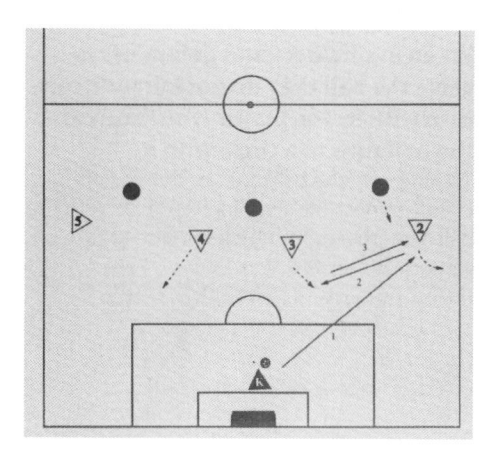

The goalkeeper (1) plays the ball out to the flank. The ball is played back to the central defender (3) or the goalkeeper, who then plays it out to the same flank again. There is no switch to the other flank.

When the goalkeeper kicks the ball out, too few players move up in support and the center is insufficiently covered.

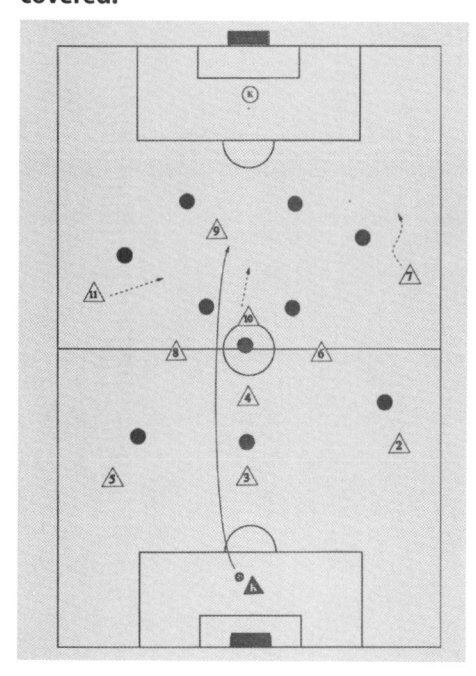

The goalkeeper (1) kicks the ball out. The defenders and midfielders move forward very little or not at all. The right and left backs (2 and 5) do not move inside. This means that there is more space between the lines and between the individual defenders.

After the ball is won, it is immediately lost again.

After pressure is put on the ball in the penalty area, the defensive midfielder gains possession. He runs with the ball toward the center line. His teammates move up to support him. The defensive midfielder is not comfortable on the ball and immediately loses possession. His first pass after he wins the ball goes to an opponent. The defense is often vulnerable immediately after winning possession.

The midfielders are not involved in the build-up play.

The primary aim of build-up play from the back is to get the ball forward to the attackers. In practice this is not always possible. The next option is then to play the ball to the midfielders. Too often, this option is not used in youth soccer. This can hold back the development of defenders and midfielders.

The midfielders take too many risks and lose the ball too often. They are not sufficiently careful.

When the ball crosses the center line, all the players try to get forward. The defensive organization is vulnerable. In this situation, loss of possession must be avoided.

The left and/or the right midfielder play too far forward.

Midfielders who play too far forward unbalance the team. Sometimes they are so far forward that they are not available to receive a pass. Midfielders have to support the attackers. When they play too far forward they cannot fulfill this role and it is more difficult to get the ball to the attackers.

5

Book 1   Build-Up Play

Technique-related aspects

Receiving the ball

When midfielders and defenders receive the ball they do not immediately turn with it. The player who receives the ball runs in a circle with it.
Turning with the ball must be done as efficiently as possible. Running in a circle with the ball gives the opposing player time to take up a new position.

As the defender tries to turn with the ball he lets it run past him. This gives the attacker a chance to win the ball.

The defender makes himself available to receive the ball when he is facing his goal.
The defender has to turn through 180 degrees when he receives the ball. He cannot see where the opposing players are.

The ball is not under control.
A player must control the ball with his first touch so that he can pass or go immediately after receiving it.

The ball is stationary too often
A stationary ball is an easy prey for the opposition.

Section 1 - Work Items

Goalkeeping-related aspects

The goalkeeper loses too much time when he receives the ball.
Goalkeepers sometimes take a few steps backward when they receive the ball. Instead of moving forward to receive the ball and then pushing it forward, he stops the ball and takes a few steps back before moving forward again to kick the ball into play. This takes too much time and gives the opposition time to put pressure on the ball.

When the goalkeeper takes a goal kick, the players make themselves available too early to receive the ball.
The goalkeeper places the ball for the goal kick. As soon as he looks up, the players make themselves available to receive the ball. This forces the goalkeeper to play the ball too soon, often with poor results.

The goalkeeper fails to take up a new position after playing the ball.

The goalkeeper plays the ball and stays where he is. This robs the player who receives the ball of the option of passing it back to the goalkeeper.

> "If a goalkeeper has a lot of space in front of him when his team is in possession, he must move up to guard this space, or the defensive line must fall back."
>
> *Sef Vergoosen*

The goalkeeper kicks the ball out aimlessly
The goalkeeper takes the ball to the edge of the penalty area and kicks it aimlessly upfield.

The goalkeeper fails to signal that he is going to kick the ball long.
The goalkeeper unexpectedly kicks a long ball forward. The players need time to move up to support their attackers.

The goalkeeper chooses the wrong kicking technique.
The goalkeeper tries to kick the ball out accurately, but chooses the wrong kicking technique.

The goalkeeper fails to communicate a message with the ball.
The speed and path of the ball and the direction of the play are not adjusted to suit the situation.

Example 1
The central defender calls for the ball from the goalkeeper. The opposing attacker is nearby, but there is just enough space to play the ball to a defender. The goalkeeper sends the ball ahead of the defender, thus putting him in a difficult situation.

Example 2
The full back has space in front of him, but the goalkeeper plays the ball to his feet.

Book 1   Build-Up Play

Aspects of facing a team with 3 strikers

The central defender (3) and the defensive midfielder (4) stay too close to each other.

The central defender (3) and the defensive midfielder (4) take up positions to receive the ball, but stand too close to each other. This gives the striker (9) the chance to pressure the player in possession.

When the ball is played to one of the two central players, the other remains in line with him.

The central defender (3) has the ball and has no option for playing the ball forward into an attacking zone. The striker (9) puts pressure on the opposing players. The defensive midfielder (4) stays square of the central defender and is therefore difficult to pass to.

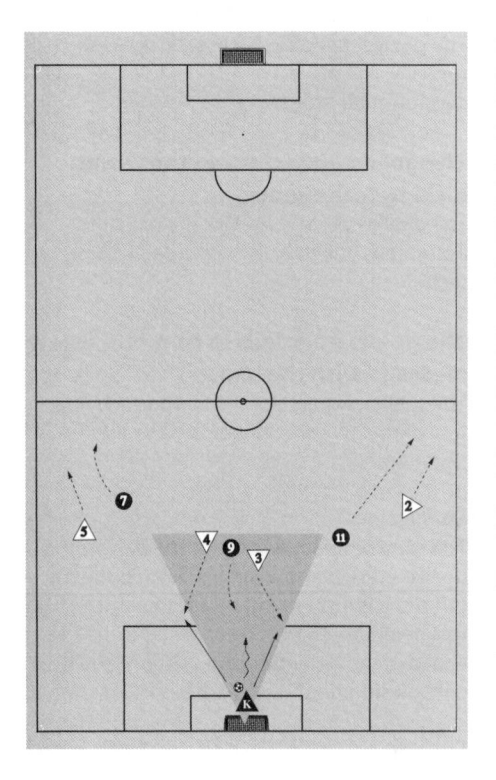

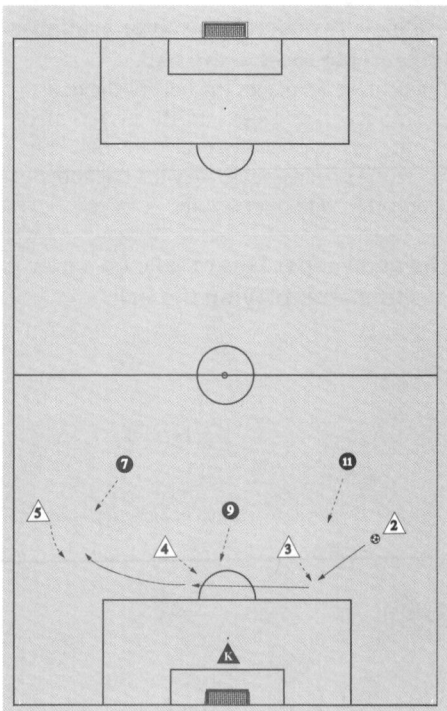

Section 1 - Work Items

Aspects of facing a team with 2 strikers

Both central players make themselves available to receive the ball.
Both central players (3 and 4) make themselves available to receive the ball and take their direct opponents with them. There is therefore less space on the flanks and the goalkeeper has fewer passing options.

The right or left fullback (2 and 5) calls for the ball and falls back too far.
The right or left fullback (2 and 5) calls for the ball in the corner of the field, where the opposition can exert pressure more easily.

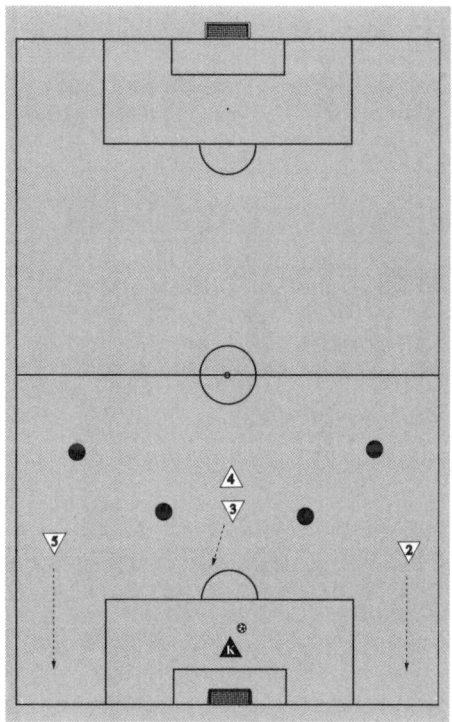

Book 1 Build-Up Play

Section 2 - Tasks and Functions

Tasks and functions

Book 1   Build-Up Play

Tasks and functions

I have chosen a 1-3-4-3 system, to which I have linked a way of playing. Within each system and the associated way of playing, there are tasks and functions for the team as a whole, the lines (defense, midfield, attack) and the individual positions. The tasks and functions in this description are totally oriented to the development of young soccer players.

Age plays a key role here. The tasks and functions differ for each age group. The tasks and functions described here are aimed at 15 to 18-year-olds. Coaches of other age groups can integrate those tasks and functions that are suitable for their own players.

Where it is specified that players must not lose possession in their own half, this must be understood in context. Clearly, loss of possession must be avoided. However, not losing possession is not an objective in its own right. Young players must be able to develop as many skills as possible. If we take the comment "no loss of possession" literally, this strangles the players' development options. A young player must be able to experiment. Trying out new fakes and techniques is part of this. The approach to the tasks and functions must be aligned to age-related objectives and age-typical characteristics. There must be room for experimentation. If we forbid the central defender from pushing forward into midfield, for example, we prevent him from developing a number of skills. The tasks and functions described here are more a framework for the coach than a target to be achieved.

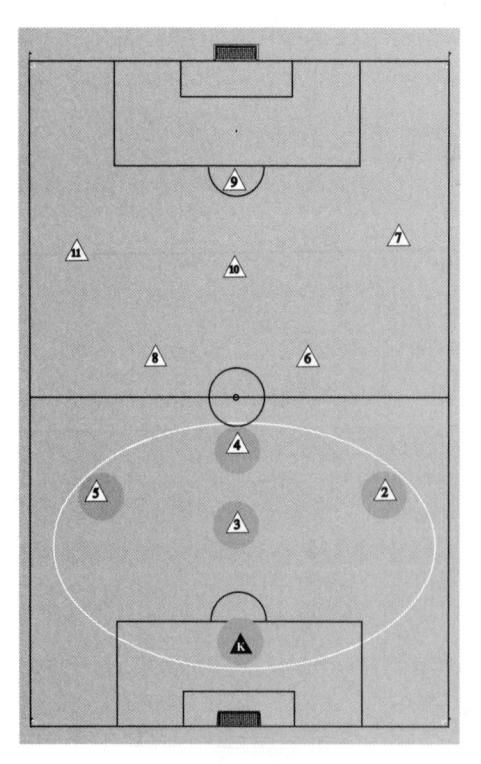

Tasks for the whole team (build-up)
- Make the playing area as large as possible (length and width).
- Don't stand too close together or too far apart.
- Positional play should be aimed at getting the ball forward into attacking zones.
- Good link-up play between the lines in the forward build-up.
- Don't stand too far apart.
- Stay focused.

Tasks for the individual lines (build-up)
Defensive line
- No unnecessary loss of possession in your own half.
- Keep the ball circulating quickly.
- Try to switch the play as quickly as possible.
- Try to play the ball forward as quickly as possible.
- Try to play the ball to teammates in space.
- Take up good positions relative to your teammates.
- Use the space well relative to the opposing team's strikers.
- Communicate!

Section 2 - Tasks and Functions

Midfield line
- Read the game.
- Avoid losing possession in your own half.
- Try to play the ball to teammates in space.
- Take up positions that allow the ball to be played forward into attacking zones, or take up positions where you can receive the ball.
- Don't run too much with the ball.
- Support your strikers.
- Fast play (one-touch play – good ball control – take up good positions).

Attacking line
- Take up positions that allow the ball to be played forward into attacking zones.
- Good movement (run toward the ball, then check away).
- Keep the playing area as large as possible (wingers stay on the flank).
- Vary your runs into space so they are not predictable.
- Don't move toward the ball too early.

Tasks by position (build-up)
Goalkeeper (1)
- Direct your teammates!
- Participate in the positional play.
- Take up positions where you are available.
- Try to anticipate the play.
- Be aware of what is happening at the other end of the field and play the ball to your attackers if you can.
- Try to ensure that your team keeps possession.
- Take no risks in the vicinity of your goal.
- Make sure you can react adequately if your team loses possession.
- Ensure good communication.

Central defender (3)
- Direct your teammates!
- Be aware of what is happening in the attacking zone and play the ball to your attackers if you can.
- Important role in switching the ball from one side of the field to the other.
- Make sure a backpass is always possible.
- Good cooperation with the defensive midfielder (4).
- Don't take up positions on the same level as the defensive midfielder.
- Support the right and left backs (2 and 5).

Defensive midfielder (4)
- Take up positions where you are available.
- Take up positions in front of the defensive line.
- Don't run too much with the ball.
- Important role in switching the ball from one side of the field to the other.
- Take up good positions relative to the ball.
- Support your teammates.
- Take up positions that enable you to cover quickly if the team loses possession.

Right and left backs (2 and 5)
- Important role in positional play – try to drag strikers away in order to create space.
- Fan out toward the flanks.
- Be ready to react quickly if possession is lost.
- Be aware of what is happening in the attacking zone and play the ball to your attackers if you can.
- Look out for opportunities to pass the ball forward into attacking zones.
- Keep possession if build-up down the flank is not possible.

Midfielders (6 and 8)
- Try to create opportunities to pass the ball forward into attacking zones.
- Support the strikers.
- One of the midfielders must be ready to cover quickly if possession is lost.
- Do not make a forward run too quickly.
- Keep the play under control.
- Focus on creating chances.
- Be available to receive the ball from the back.

Book 1   Build-Up Play

Section 3 - The Aims of the Game

The aims of the game

Book 1   Build-Up Play

The aims of the game

Build-up

The game of soccer can be broken down into 3 situations: own team in possession, opposing team in possession, and change of possession. Possession can in turn be broken down into 2 phases:
- **Build-up**
- **Attack**

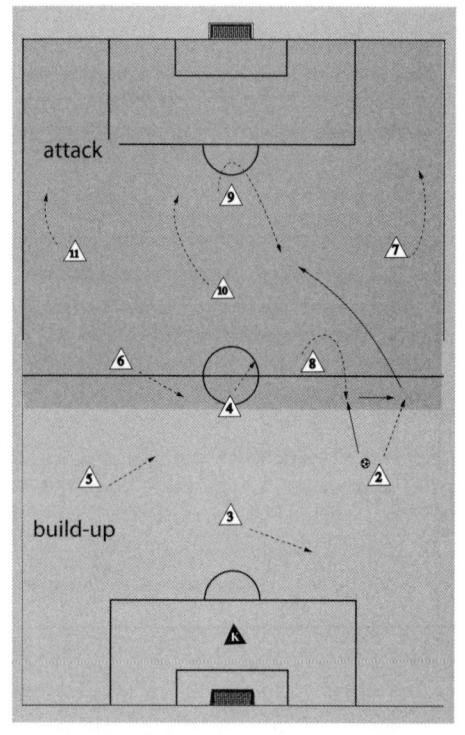

The aims of the game must be translated into practice to promote the individual development of the players rather than just to get a result.

The aims of build-up play are to find a player in space by circulating the ball, and to create opportunities to pass the ball forward into attacking zones. It is important for a team not to lose possession near its own goal.

To achieve these aims we must clearly explain what build-up play involves. In this section we give some pointers for the key build-up players (the goalkeeper and the defenders in cooperation with the midfielders and attackers). The aims must be translated into practice with the focus on furthering the players' development.

We explain the most common aims of the game and the principles of build-up play.

Build-up options for the goalkeeper
- Pass to the attackers or into space.
- Pass to the midfielders.
- Pass to the defenders.
- Kick the ball into play.
- Goal kick.

Build-up option for the defenders
- Pass to the attackers (into space or to feet)
- Pass to the midfielders.
- Pass to another defender.

Attacking is about creating chances in the opposing team's half. The players try to open up the defense and score goals.

The build-up is the preparation for the attack. The players try to get the ball forward purposefully and efficiently. Build-up play from the back takes place in the team's own half and around the center circle.

> "I also said that if we are in possession and we can play the ball forward down the middle, we don't pass it square or back. That is the starting point, and everyone has to be aware of it."
>
> *Sef Vergoossen*

Section 3 - The Aims of the Game

The aims of build-up play

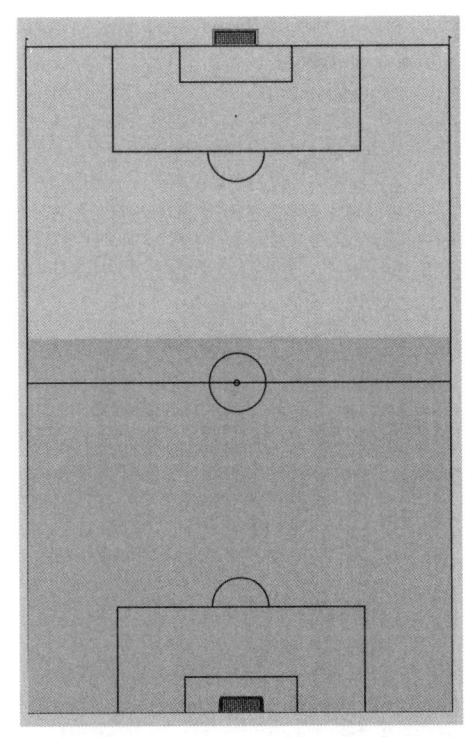

Aims:
- Finding a player in space by circulating the ball.
- Playing the ball forward into an attacking zone as quickly as possible

By:
- Good positional play
- Rapid ball circulation

Build-up play from the back can be divided into 2 situations:

Build-up play against a disorganized team
If the opposing team is disorganized, it is important to play the ball forward into an attacking zone as quickly as possible. When an attack breaks down, the team needs a few seconds to reorganize.

Build-up play against an organized team
In this case the players involved in the build-up play must be more patient. They must wait for the right moment to play the ball forward.

The goalkeeper's build-up options

When the goalkeeper has the ball, he must be aware of what is happening at the other end of the field and must play the ball to his team's attackers if he can. Because the opposing team's goal is at the other end of the field, we have to get there as efficiently as possible. The player with the ball has to choose from the following options:

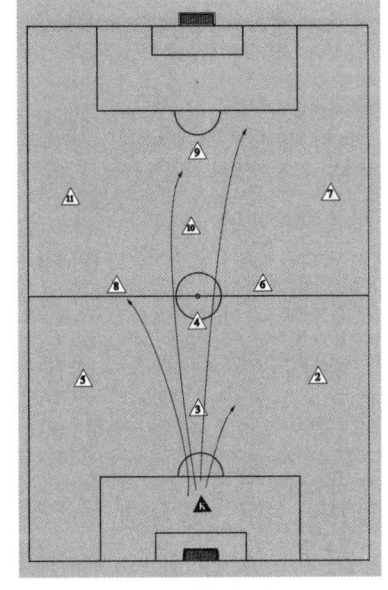

1. Play the ball into space between the attackers and the opposing team's goal.
2. Play the ball down the middle to the attackers.
3. Play the ball down the middle to the midfielders.
4. Play the ball down the middle to the defenders.
5. Play the ball wide to the full backs.

The choice of option depends on the players. The aim is to gain ground as quickly as possible. If an attacker is accessible in the space between the defenders and their goal, this will be the first choice. During Louis van Gaal's successful period as the coach of Ajax Amsterdam, for example, Ajax goalkeeper Edwin van der Sar would send the ball quickly forward to the sprinting Mark Overmars. However, this solution is not always available. In youth soccer, keeping possession is one of the most important lessons. Simply getting the ball forward quickly is not good for the development of build-up play. It is therefore often better to choose a short-passing option (goalkeeper – defenders – midfielders).

Book 1   Build-Up Play

The Keeper

The goalkeeper can kick or throw the ball. What he chooses to do often depends on his personality or the influence of the coaching staff. One possibility is as follows:

- In the first phase, he chooses to play the ball forward into an attacking zone. Depending on the position and skill of the player, he might drop-kick, volley or throw the ball.
- If the above option is not feasible, he tries to start the build-up by play by passing to a defender or a midfielder.
- He then places the ball on the ground at his feet.
- Depending on the available options, the goalkeeper can opt for a short-passing build-up via defenders and midfielders, or play a long-ball forward.

This approach has a number of advantages, and is especially effective with players aged 6 to 16.

- The ball-playing skills of the goalkeeper are improved.
- The goalkeeper is immediately on the ball. Rolling the ball forward and then kicking it demands a switch from the goalkeeper.

> "Youth team players can win; adult players must win."
>
> *Gerry Mühren*
> *Former professional soccer player with Ajax Amsterdam, Seville, etc.*

Pass from the goalkeeper to the attackers in free space

Not every age group can start the build-up play in this way. In view of their limited action radius, players in the 11 to 14 age group will have difficulties with this option. The way the ball is played depends on the skills of the goalkeeper, the skills of the attackers and the available space. The goalkeeper can play the ball out as follows.

a) A targeted pass to the feet of an attacker
The ball can be played to the feet or chest of an attacker if the opposition is not as well organized as it should be. The runs by the midfielders are crucial here. By taking defenders with them towards their own goal, they create space for a targeted pass to the attackers. The ball can be kicked from the ground, thrown or drop-kicked.

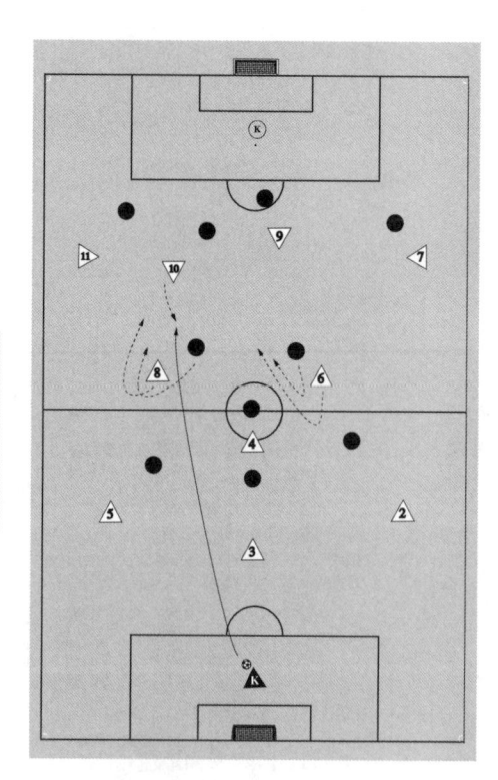

Section 3 - The Aims of the Game

b) A targeted high ball and the creation of a 1v1 situation

If no teammates are free, the goalkeeper can send a long ball upfield. He can do this when:
- The opposing team plays man-to-man defense.
- No other options are available and the goalkeeper is put under pressure.
- An attacker is strong in the air and has a good chance of winning a heading duel.
- The goalkeeper has deficits in his technique.

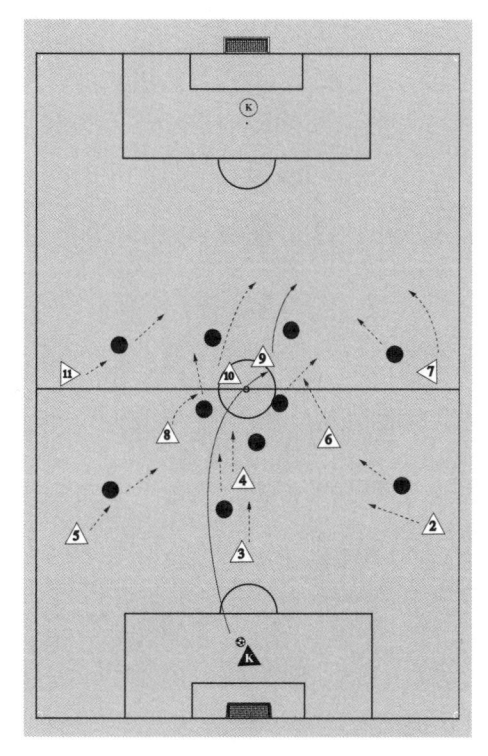

Results are soon forgotten!
When you are 18 you don't care what results you achieved when you were 12.

The important thing is to gain possession of the loose ball. The other attackers and midfielders who have made a forward run can play a decisive role in gaining and keeping possession of the ball after a heading duel. The goalkeeper can use one of several techniques, such as a long kick from the ground, a drop-kick, etc.

c) Long ball into free space

This is possible in a limited number of situations. Not every goalkeeper can kick the ball 60 yards, so the individual skills of the goalkeeper are crucial. . This tactical choice is possible for 15 to 18 year-olds. It can be used when the opposing team takes more risks and plays man-to-man defense. A ball into free space can have a surprise effect after the opposing team takes a corner or a free-kick. The best headers of the ball in the opposing team's defense often go forward in such situations and their roles are taken over by players with less experience in these positions. If the goalkeeper wins the ball and immediately sends a long ball forward, this can create dangerous situations.

Pass from goalkeeper to midfielders

Passing to the midfielders requires good technique. The available space is often limited. Midfielders only have enough space to receive a pass if the opposition is less well organized than usual. In the example shown, the goalkeeper (1) catches the ball at the near post. He then throws the ball to the unmarked midfielder (6), who is making a diagonal run to create space to receive the ball. In view of the freedom of movement the goalkeeper has in the penalty area, this situation is a possibility in any youth soccer match. From midfield, it is easy for young players to set up an attack.

"Some players always kick the ball perfectly during practice sessions. During a match, though, they only achieve 60 percent. There is a great difference in efficiency between practice and real matches."

Franky Van der Elst

Book 1   Build-Up Play

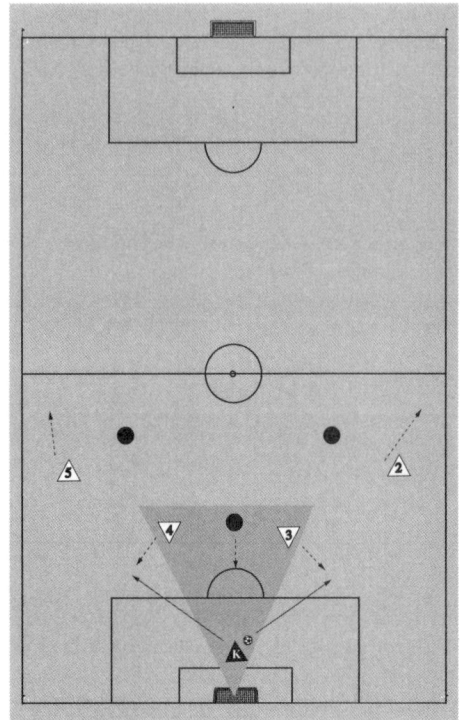

"Soccer is about expressing yourself in an organized team context."

Roger Lemerre
(coach of the French national team)

Pass from goalkeeper to defenders

The opposing team plays with 3 attackers:
We try to exploit the numerical advantage in the center. The right and left backs (2 and 5) take up positions further forward on the flanks and try to tempt their opponents to go with them. This creates a 2 against 1 situation in the center (striker against 2 central defenders). The 2 defenders stand further apart and call for the ball. When they receive the ball they turn to look forward.

The central defenders receive the ball from the goalkeeper (receive and go)
- The defender stands diagonally to the path of the ball to receive it

It is important that the defender does not get the ball under his body when he receives it. He must be able to turn with the ball. A central defender cannot usually allow the ball to roll past him. The positions of the opposing strikers are crucial here.

The defenders try to play the ball past the central striker as quickly as possible and create an extra-man situation. When the defenders play the ball to each other, the striker has to make a decision. The pass to the other defender must be firm. Playing the ball diagonally forward, sometimes past the striker, gives the other

Section 3 - The Aims of the Game

How far the 4 players fall back depends on the opposition.

defender the space to shake off the striker. A change of pace might be sufficient to escape from the striker (Fig. 1). If the ball is played square, the striker has time to turn and put pressure on the other defender (Fig. 2).

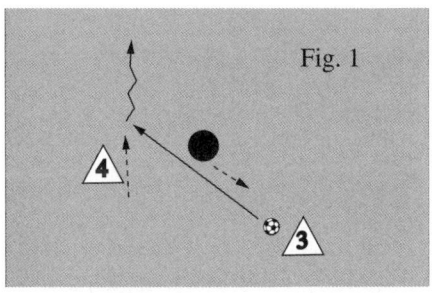

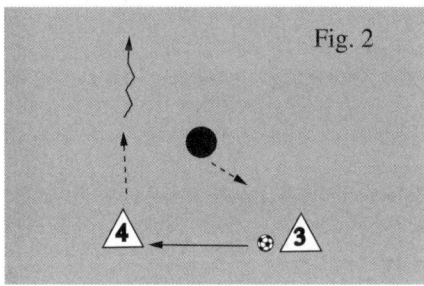

Fig. 1

Fig. 2

The same principles apply to passing to the right or left backs; the aim is to create an extra-man situation in midfield. We try to pass the ball as far forward as possible to the full back, and as firmly as possible past the opposing player (in this case as close as possible to the outside left of the opposing team).

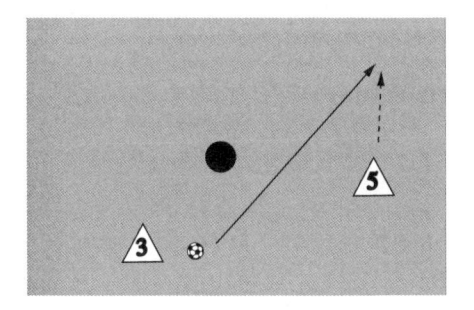

"The aim of build-up play is to create an extra-man situation in midfield."

Hein Van Haezebrouck

Opposing team plays with 2 attackers

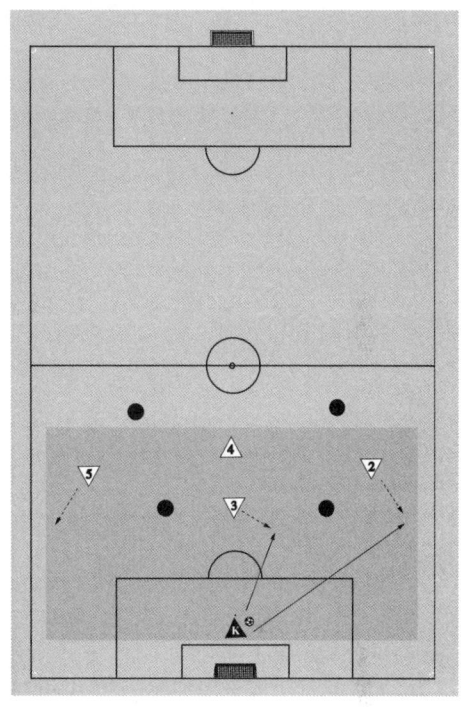

The 2 attackers generally take up positions around an imaginary line down the center of the field. This means that there is more space on the flanks. If the opposing team plays with 2 strikers, the players on the wing will probably be midfielders rather than attackers. This means that they will be reluctant to get too far forward to put pressure on the build-up players. There is therefore more space on the flanks, and it will therefore be easier to pass to the right and left backs (2 and 5). In the center it is important that only one player (the central defender) makes himself available to receive the ball. In this way a 4 against 2 situation is created (the central defender (3), the left and right backs (2 and 5) and the goalkeeper (1) against the 2 opposing strikers).

Allowing defenders to push forward with the ball improves their skills.

Book 1   Build-Up Play

Full backs should be moving forward when they make themselves available. Some full backs call for the ball when they are moving back. This wastes time (Fig. 1). The full back should create space and run onto the ball (Fig. 2).

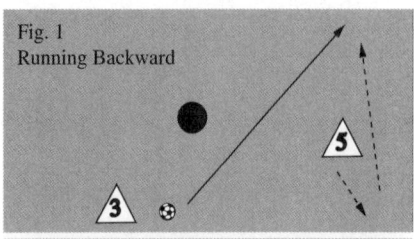

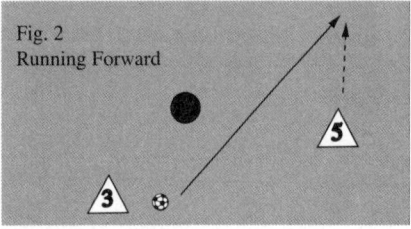

Fig. 1
Running Backward

Fig. 2
Running Forward

Coaching the goalkeeper
- When you receive the ball, choose the most attacking option.
- Communicate with your teammates.
- Use both feet.
- Try to play the ball out in such a way that the receiver can control it easily.
- Try to play the ball into space in front of the receiver rather than to his feet.
- Communicate with the receiver.
- The goalkeeper has a number of options when he is in possession of the ball.
  a) Aim the ball into the space behind the opposing team's defenders.
  b) Play the ball to the attackers (into space in front of them or firmly at the body).
  c) Play the ball to an advanced midfield player.
  d) Play the ball to an advanced defender.
  e) Just kick the ball forward without any specific aim.
  f) Kick the ball out of play over the sideline.
  g) Concede a corner.

After playing the ball
- Watch the play closely and position yourself accordingly.
- Communicate with your teammates.
- Make sure your teammates can play the ball back to you if necessary.

Be aware of what is happening in the attacking zone and play the ball to your attackers if you can.

Coaching the full backs
a) Making yourself available
- Try to create space for your teammates.
- Keep moving.
- Adapt continuously to the game situation.
- Keep your back to the sideline; align yourself to the opposing team's goal.

b) Receiving the ball
- Control the ball with your outside foot.
- Stay aware of the game situation.
- Don't stand still as you receive the ball.
- Create space for yourself – make sure your teammates can play the ball into the space in front of you.

c) Passing
- Try to play the ball from outside to inside.
- Play the ball into the attacking zone if possible.
- Try not to lose possession.
- Move forward immediately to link up with the other defenders after passing.
- Communicate with the player in possession.

d) When the ball is passed to a teammate
- Immediately adjust your position to the play.
- Ensure that you are available to receive the ball.
- Communicate with the player in possession.
  - If a teammate passes the ball into the attacking zone, move forward immediately in support.

Coaching the central defender
a) Getting into position to receive the ball.
- If you make a run, do it with conviction.
- Be aware of the positions of the attackers.
- Communicate with your teammates.

b) Receive and go
- Use both feet to control the ball.
- Stay aware of the game situation as you receive the ball.
- Stay aware of your defensive responsibilities.
- Avoid unnecessary loss of possession.

Too little attention is paid to coaching the goalkeeper to use his weaker foot.

Section 3 - The Aims of the Game

c) Passing
- Play the ball into the attacking zone if possible.
- Try not to lose possession.
- Try to play the ball from inside to outside.
- Move forward immediately to link up with the other defenders after passing.
- Communicate with the player in possession.

d) When the ball is passed to a teammate
- Immediately adjust your position to the play.
- Ensure that you are available to receive the ball.
- Communicate with the player in possession.
- If a teammate passes the ball into the attacking zone, move forward immediately in support.

Simply booting the ball upfield might stop the opposition from scoring a goal, but it does nothing for the development of soccer ability.

How the goalkeeper kicks the ball into play

In general, little attention is focused on how young goalkeepers kick the ball into play (drop kick, volley, etc.). The goalkeeper often simply kicks the ball without giving much thought to it. It is important for goalkeepers to learn from a young age to make conscious choices in how they use the ball. The goalkeeper can direct a high ball toward an attacker who is strong in the air, or play it into space (not suitable at a very young age) or play it into the path of a fast runner. Players aged 15 to 18 can learn about other tactical options.

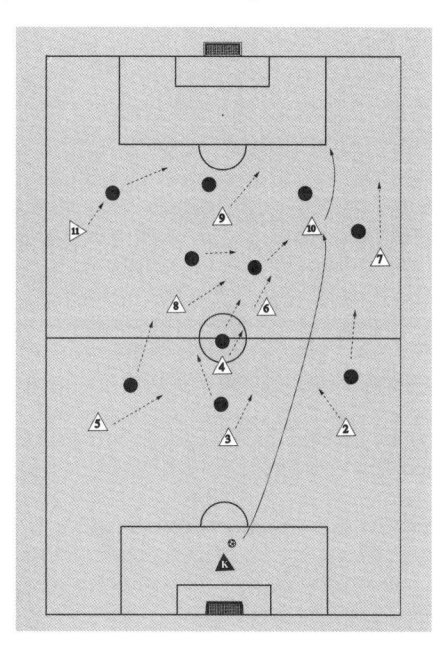

If the goalkeeper directs his kick between the central defender and the full back, he makes life harder for the opposing team.
- The other central defender can provide less cover, as he must remain in the center.
- The ball can be directed toward the flank where the central defender who is less strong in the air is positioned.
- A winger and a midfielder are nearby to profit from the loose ball.

Goal kick

The limited range of the youngest players is the main obstacle to playing 11v11. Even working the ball out of the penalty area is a major task for 10 to 12 year-olds. We are in favor of allowing goal kicks to be taken from the edge of the penalty area (across the whole width of the penalty area) in this age group. This gives the goalkeeper the opportunity to carry out goal kicks at his own level. Goal kicks should be taken quickly. This gives the opposition less time to organize and hold up the build-up play. However, if the opposition does close down the goalkeeper's options, in the older age groups the goalkeeper can choose to play a targeted long ball forward. Younger goalkeepers may not yet have the technique or the strength to do this. It is not advisable to allow a field player to take the goal kick instead of the goalkeeper. This will not help him to improve his technique and coordination. Taking the kick quickly can partially solve the problem. A goalkeeper with deficient ball playing skills should be integrated into training sessions as a field player as often as possible. This, in combination with homework (kicking practice) can quickly improve the situation.

Defenders are often too quick to call for the ball from the goalkeeper. A goalkeeper must have the time to control the ball before he kicks it. If he plays the ball too hastily, possession is often lost.

Book 1   Build-Up Play

The backpass
In the case of very young players (aged 8 to 12), the goalkeeper can play as the last man. This means that he has more ball contacts and his soccer ability is stimulated. From the age of about 12, his tasks can be changed. A goalkeeper of this age must be able to carry out his tasks and functions and make his own contribution. He takes up positions a long way in front of his goal, but can adjust his position to suit the play. There is more focus on not conceding goals. From age 15 to 18 the match result becomes more important and has more elements of adult soccer. Goalkeepers should learn how to use both feet from their youngest years.

Tips for the players
- Pass to the goalkeeper as quickly as possible.
- Try to make it easy for the goalkeeper to control the ball (play it along the ground).
- Pass to both feet.
- After passing to the goalkeeper, get into space so that the goalkeeper can pass back to you.
- Communicate with the goalkeeper.
- Vary the pace of the ball to suit the situation.
- Ensure that the goalkeeper can deal with the ball directly.

Tips for the goalkeeper
- Try not to take any risks.
- Try to decide what you are going to do as soon as possible (before the ball reaches you).
- Decide whether to control the ball and go, or to pass it with your first touch.
- Take the ball past an opponent only for the purpose of getting into space.
- Adjust your position as quickly as possible to developments in the play (be available to receive the ball; ensure that you can defend the goal as well as possible).
- Focus on the path and speed of the ball.
- The goalkeeper has a number of options:
  a) Play the ball into the space behind the opposing team's defenders.
  b) Play the ball to the attackers.
  c) Play the ball to an advanced midfield player.
  d) Play the ball to an advanced defender.
  e) Kick the ball forward into the attacking zone.
  f) Kick the ball out of play over the sideline.
  g) Concede a corner.

Goalkeeper receives the ball
When the goalkeeper receives the ball, he must be aware of the positions of the opposing players.

Examples
Situation 1: Opponent leaves a lot of space

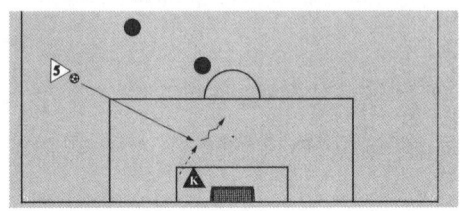

The goalkeeper has plenty of space to take the ball diagonally forward. He can therefore pass it in any direction.

Situation 2: Opposing player is nearby

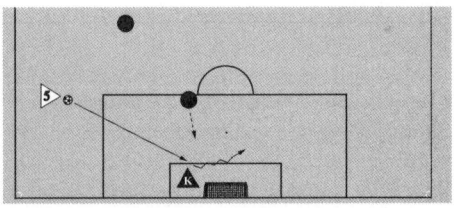

The goalkeeper turns away from the opposing player as he receives the ball, and takes it square. This gives him more space to move with the ball and more time to play it to a teammate.

Situation 3: Opposing player challenges for the ball

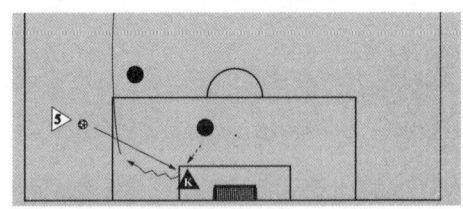

The opposing player is close to the ball. The goalkeeper cannot take it forward after receiving it. To avoid losing possession, he gains time by pushing the ball back slightly and then clears it upfield.

Situation 4: The goalkeeper has no space
In some cases the risk of losing possession is so great that the goalkeeper must clear the ball with his first touch.

Section 3 - The Aims of the Game

The defenders' build-up options

The motto "Be aware of what is happening in the attacking zone and play the ball to your attackers if you can" also applies to defenders. Above all, speed of action determines effectiveness. The urge to play the ball forward must not result in players making forward passes whenever they get the ball, and forgetting the basics of how to keep possession. The ball must not be played forward simply in the hope that something will happen. A forward pass must be based on the positions of the ball carrier's teammates and the resulting options. The following hierarchy of options applies:

1. Play the ball forward into space for the attackers.
2. Play the ball forward to the feet of an attacker.
3. Play the ball forward to the midfielders.
4. Play the ball to another defender.
5. Play the ball to the goalkeeper.

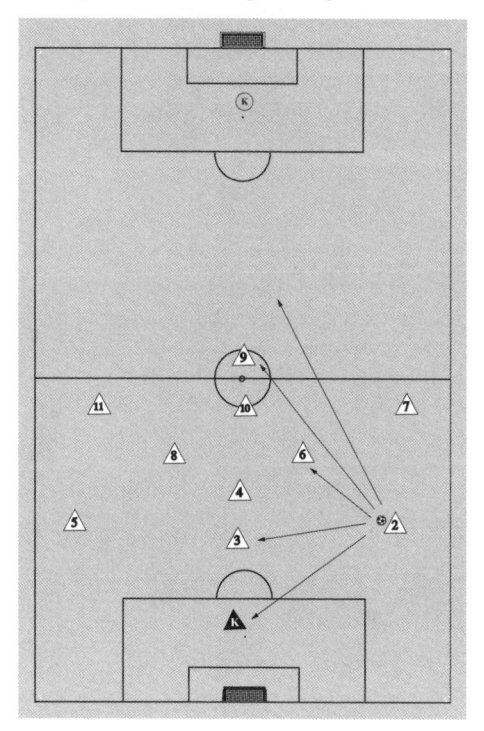

Triangles

A lot of players link up in the build-up play. In a 1-3-4-3 system, this can be represented by triangles. Thinking in triangles makes the play simpler. It gives the players more insight when another player involves them in a game situation.

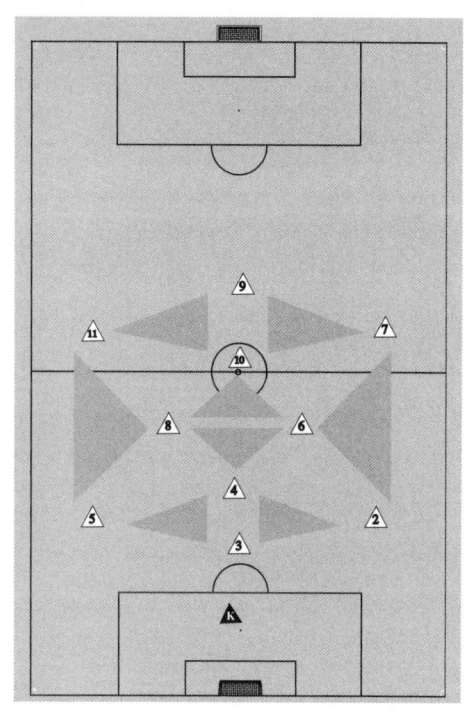

Build-up from defenders to attackers (pass into space or to feet)

Defenders must aim to get the ball into the attacking zone as quickly as possible. A fast pass from defense to attack is the starting point. How this is achieved depends on the opposing team. At one moment a fast forward pass will be possible, at another a patient build-up will be the best solution. When defenders have the ball, their first thought is to get the ball forward to the attackers, missing out the midfielders. Depending on the available space, the pass might be played to an attacker's feet or into the space behind the defense. These options are dealt with in detail in the book on attacking.

25

Book 1   Build-Up Play

Right or left back (2 or 5) plays the ball to the strikers (9 or 10)

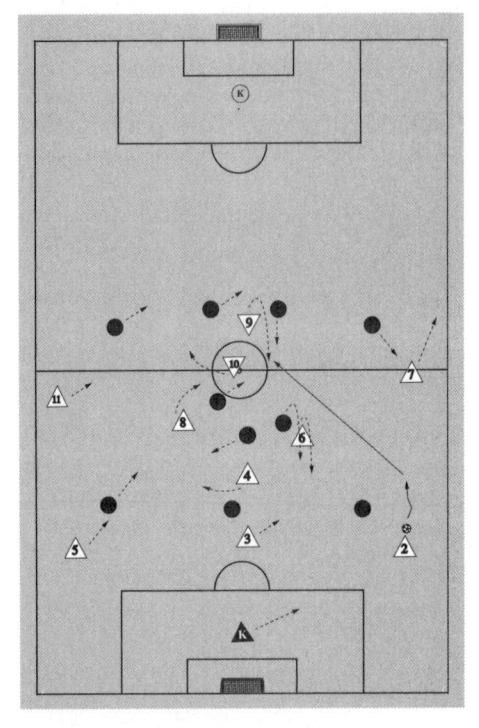

> The pace of the game is dictated by the players behind the ball.

player forward." Midfielders often delay their run until the attacker has the ball. This can slow down the play. The earlier the midfielder gets forward, the better the chance of developing the play, even if the striker (9) loses possession, because the midfielder can challenge the opposing player more quickly.

Forward passes down the flank (2/5 to 7/11) should be avoided. The opposition can defend against such a pass more easily, both collectively and individually. This option should only be used when the opposing team leaves sufficient space. If the opposing team defends too far up the field, the ball can be played behind the defender.

Central defender (3) plays the ball to the winger (7 or 11)

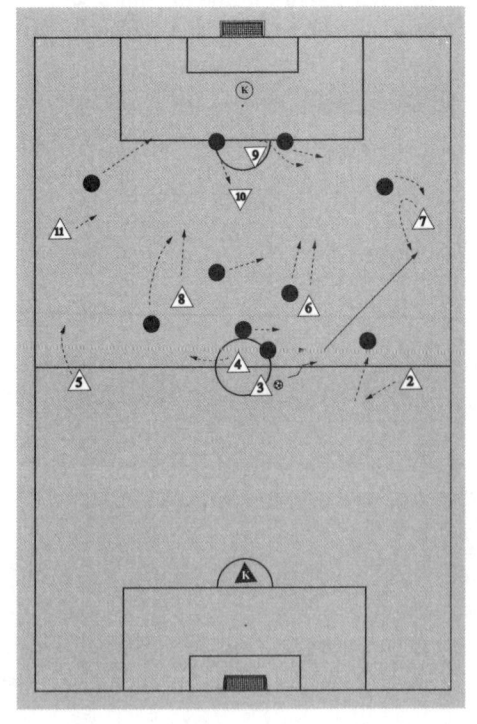

The midfield line can be missed out most easily from the full back positions (2 and 5). Preferably the ball is played to the striker (9) or the withdrawn striker (10). An important reason for this is their central position. From the center the ball can be played to either flank. When the striker or the withdrawn striker has the ball, it is more difficult for the opposing team to exert focused pressure.

The right back (2) has the ball. The right midfielder (6) drops back, thus creating space. When the right back (2) plays the ball forward, the right midfielder (6) pushes forward again to support the attackers. The supporting players must try to anticipate the play faster than the defenders. The rule is "ball forward =

> "The aim is to pass to a teammate when he is best placed, in a way that takes advantage of his strengths. In Radzinski's case the pass should be into space, in Ekakia's to his feet."
>
> *Aimé Antheunis*

Section 3 - The Aims of the Game

When a central defender has the ball, his first option is also to get the ball to the attackers, missing out the midfielders. The space created by the attackers and midfielders and the distances between the players determine what he decides to do. The ball should only be played out to the flanks if there is very little chance of it being intercepted. Such a pass requires a lot of technique and insight from the player in possession. A long ball into space is better. It is easier to play the ball to a winger with space in front of him.

The central defender (3) runs with the ball at his feet. The right midfielder (6) tries to draw his marker by making a forward run. This creates space for the central defender (3) to play the ball from the center to the right winger (7). When the central defender (3) plays the pass to the winger (7), the right midfielder (6) drops back in support.

The central defender (3) or defensive midfielder (4) switches the play to the other flank

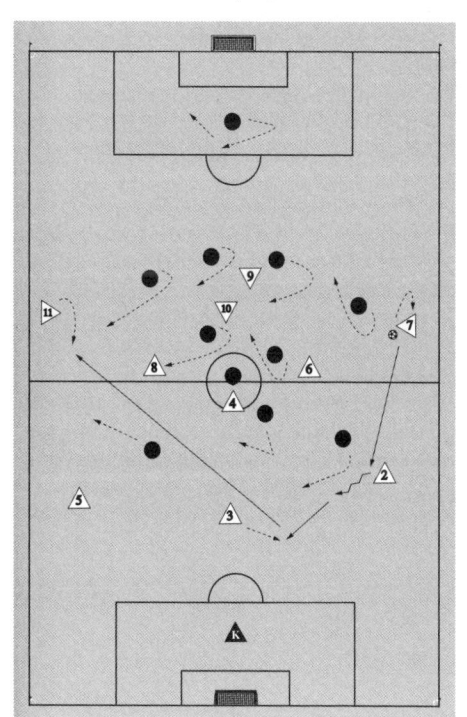

Players aged 15 to 18 have the strength and coordination to pass the ball over longer distances. A central defender (3) with good passing technique can play an important role is switching the play to the other flank.

When the central defender switches the play, the following factors are important:

- The ball must be passed to the central defender as quickly as possible. The players must therefore be able to act quickly. The opposing team must not be allowed sufficient time to reorganize when the ball is switched to the other flank
- The central defender must stay roughly midway between the sidelines. If he goes too far towards one flank, the distance to the other flank is too great to allow him to switch the play.
- The central defender must be able to send a firm pass directly to the winger.

If the central defender is right footed
In practice, the defender can best control the ball with his left foot and pass with the right.

If the central defender is left footed
Ideally the central defender should be able to play the ball comfortably with both feet. To play this technically difficult pass, the player can use his preferred foot. If he is left footed, he can control the ball with his left foot, make a half turn and pass with the left foot. The

Book 1   Build-Up Play

place where the ball is played depends on the quality of the winger and the position of his marker. The central defender must size up the situation quickly beforehand and act quickly. If his first touch is poor, or he recognizes the situation too late, things may go wrong.

Build-up from defenders to midfielders
The complexity of the midfield
The midfield positions are the most difficult on the field. In view of their central positions, midfielders have to develop a lot of insight. A midfielder must learn positional play relative to the players in front of him (attackers), players outside of him (wingers) and players behind him (defenders). They have to be aware of everything happening in the 360 degrees around them! This makes life difficult. In view of the positional requirements on midfielders, coaching in build-up play is essential. The coach must stimulate the midfielders and give them a framework that encourages them without discouraging their own individuality.

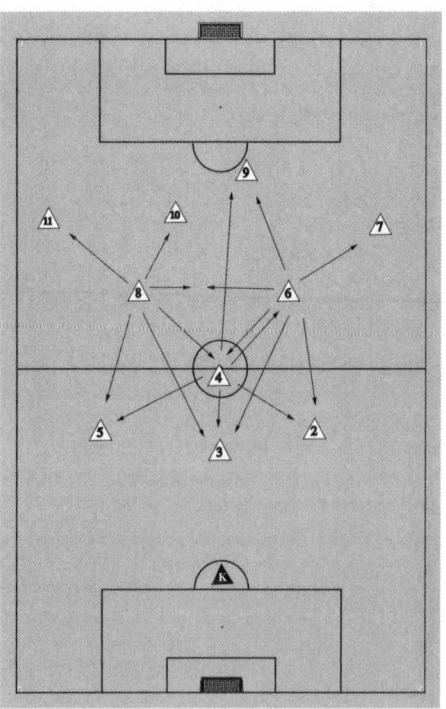

Individual requirements on midfielders in build-up play
1. They must be able to take up good positions relative to the opposing players and the ball. Through their positional play, they create more options when in possession.
2. They must make one-touch passes as often as possible.
3. They must have good ball control to allow them to create more passing options.
4. They must be able to communicate through their passes.
5. Midfielders must be able to think one or two steps ahead.
6. Midfielders must be able to maintain good positional balance relative to each other.
7. Midfielders must be able to maintain a good balance between the numbers of players in front of and behind the ball.

Collective requirements on midfielders in build-up play
Facilitate build-up play by:
- Creating space to enable the ball to be passed wide and forward.
- Supporting defenders, attackers and each other.
- Switching the play to the other flank.
- Making runs off the ball.
- Making runs with the ball.

> "Standing still in space is sometimes easier than running into space. Too many players make a run when they find themselves standing in space."
> *Jan Olde Riekerink*

Passing to a midfielder
Midfielders must try to find positions in which they are available to receive a pass. They must try to ensure they have as many options open as possible when they receive the ball. It is important how, where and when they make themselves available.

Section 3 - The Aims of the Game

General tips:
- A midfielder must know where his own players are positioned as well as the opposing team's players. This is important in the context of what to do with the ball when he receives it.
- Whether a player should check away and then back to create space to receive the ball depends on the situation. It the midfielder is in space, he does not need to create space.

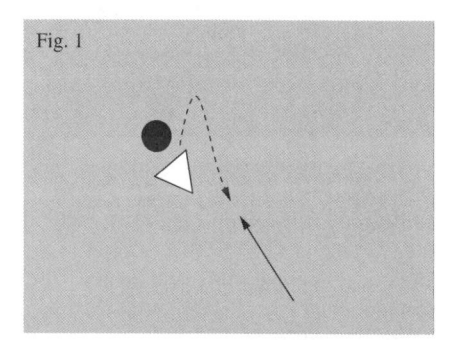

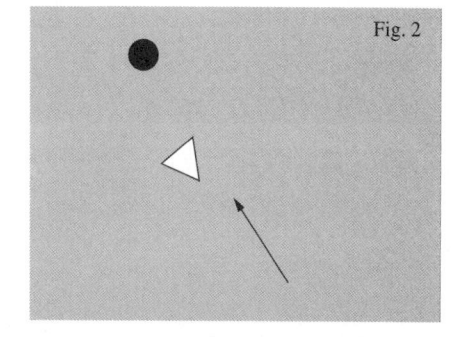

Fig. 1

Fig. 2

The midfielder is being closely marked. If he wants to escape from his marker he should check away suddenly and then check back toward the ball.

There is no marker near the midfielder. The midfielder does not need to run toward the ball or to check away and then check back toward the ball.

29

| Book 1 | Build-Up Play |

- Timing is important when a player makes himself available to receive the ball. This is often instinctive and is easier when the players have regularly played together.
Some tips:

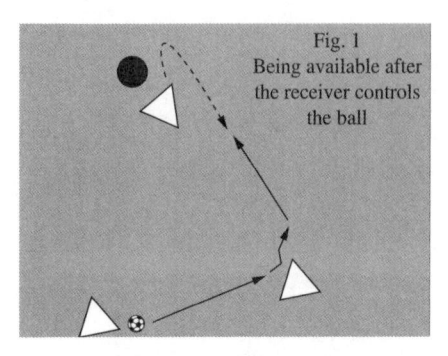

Fig. 1
Being available after the receiver controls the ball

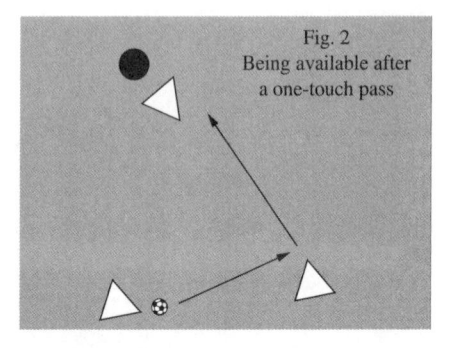

Fig. 2
Being available after a one-touch pass

The moment to shake off the marker is when the player who receives the ball has it under control and seeks eye contact with the midfielder.

In this situation the midfielder must react faster. Receiving a first-time pass requires more understanding. The direction in which the midfielder makes himself available must be clear to the passer.

- The position chosen by the midfielder must offer the most options.

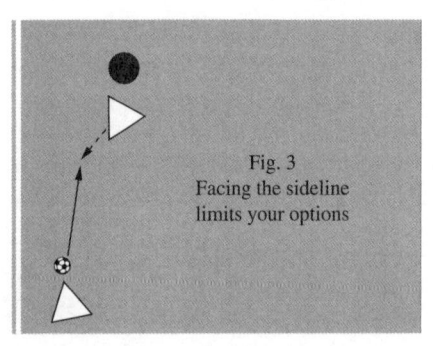

Fig. 3
Facing the sideline limits your options

By taking up a position with his face to the sideline and calling for the ball in this direction, the midfielder limits the options; the space is on the other side of the field.

- Before making himself available to receive a pass, the midfielder looks over his shoulder. He can therefore estimate the position of his marker.

"Looking over your shoulder before receiving the ball makes the continuation easier."
Franky van der Elst

Section 3 - The Aims of the Game

Receiving the ball
- The ball must be kept moving. If it is stationary, the opposition has more chance of winning it.
- The ball should be controlled in such a way that the continuation can follow naturally.
- It is not always important how the midfielder controls the ball, or with which foot. The important thing is that he controls it and takes it toward free space in one controlled movement.
- As he receives the ball, the midfielder's knees are slightly bent. His weight is mainly on the front of his feet. He can therefore react faster. This posture requires a lot of strength from the player.

The first touch must be adapted to the speed of the midfielder's run. If the midfielder sprints to the ball, he must take the speed off it more quickly than when he receives it standing still.

The midfielder (6 or 8) makes himself available to receive a pass from the right or left back (2 or 5)
Option 1: Approaching the ball diagonally.

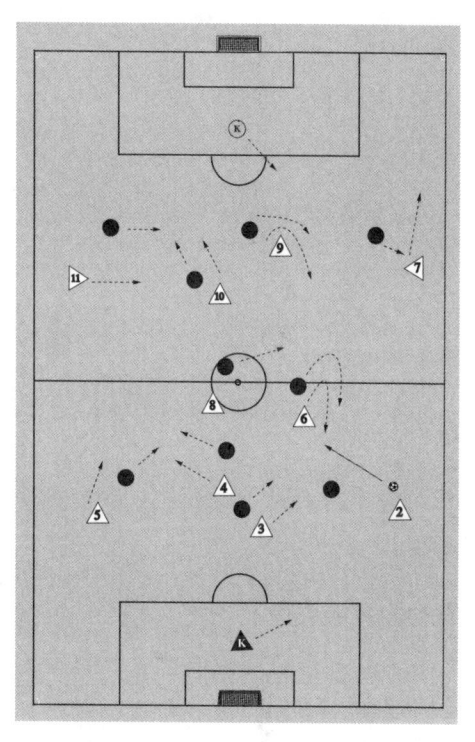

The right midfielder (6) makes a diagonal run forward and then runs into space toward the ball. He tries to form a triangle with the winger (7) and the right back (2). It is important that the midfielder runs onto the ball at an angle. The marker must decide whether to follow him or not. If he doesn't, the midfielder is free and can turn with ball.

> "Playing too many one-twos is a way of avoiding responsibility"
>
> *Aimé Antheunis*

31

Book 1   Build- Up Play

Diagonal run toward the ball.

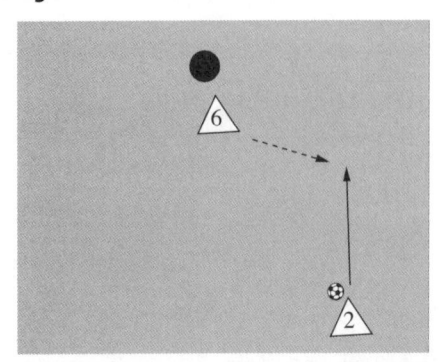

Straight run toward the ball

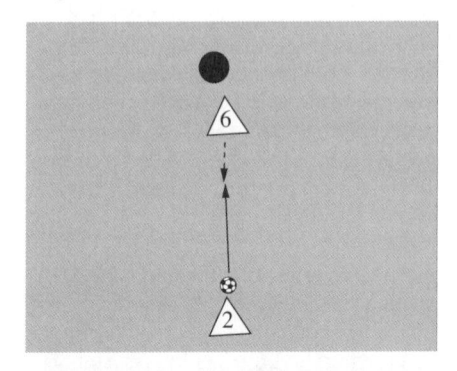

This way of making yourself available is easier to defend against. The midfielder is at an angle to the path of the ball as he receives it. If the situation allows, he uses the outside foot to receive the ball (first touch) and the inside foot to go (second touch). If he is in space he need not check away and check back to create space, but can turn immediately with the ball. The midfielder must maintain the distance between himself and the right back (2). If he comes too far to receive the ball, he has more distance to cover when he turns and has fewer options.

"Take up positions so that you run onto the ball at an angle to its path."

Franky van der Elst

Section 3 - The Aims of the Game

In principle, we try to play the ball as far forward as possible. We try to pass to the advanced midfielder so that he can turn with the ball. Depending on where the defender is positioned, the ball is played into space for him to run forward onto, or to his feet, or into space for him to run back onto. Correct coaching is essential.

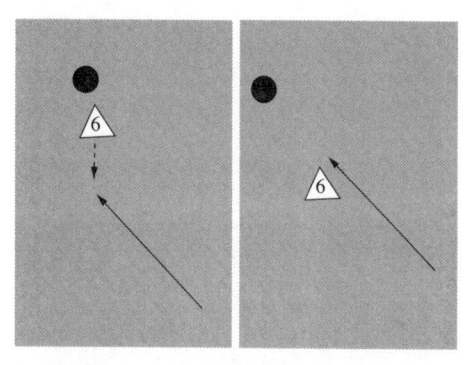

Midfielders must not make runs too far forward, as this can make them difficult to reach.

> "The midfielders of Manchester United are given very specific coaching about turning with the ball when they receive it. During training sessions, the player must turn with the ball when he receives it. If he cannot turn, he must play it back. Look at Paul Scholes. Every time he receives a pass he looks over his shoulder to see where his marker is. If he cannot turn, he passes the ball back."
>
> *Mick Priest*
> *Manchester United*

Option 2: Make a run from behind your opponent

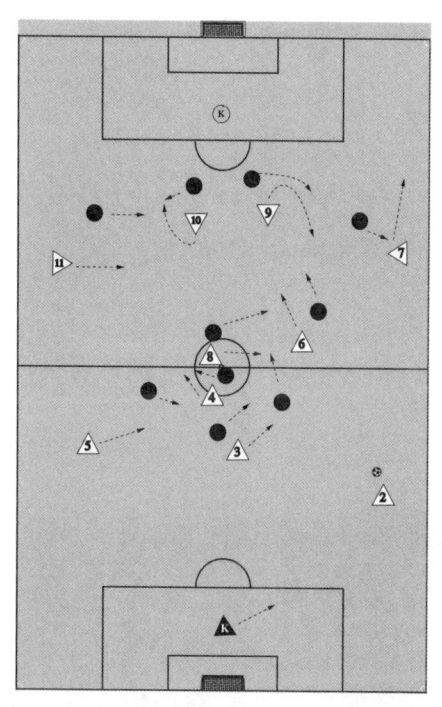

The right back (2) has the ball. The right midfielder (6) makes a forward run to get behind the opposing player.

Book 1   Build-Up Play

There are 2 options:

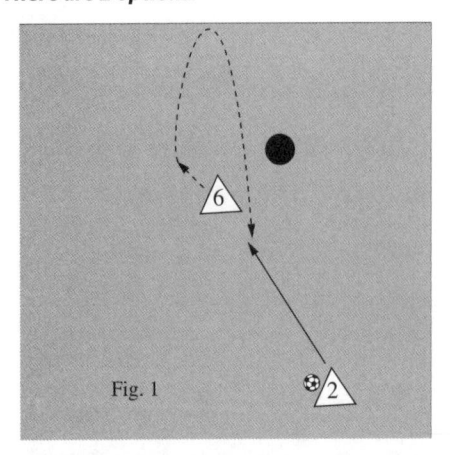

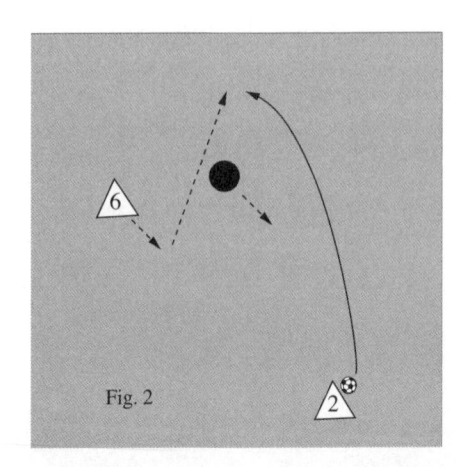

Fig. 1

Fig. 2

The midfielder (6) checks away to get behind the opposing player. If the opposing player is watching the ball, the midfielder (6) calls for it. During the few seconds when the midfielder (6) is out of the field of vision of the opposing player, he gains a few yards advantage. He therefore has a few yards' head start when he receives the ball (Fig. 1).

If the opposing player goes too far toward the ball carrier, the midfielder (6) can make a run behind his back. If he does this a few times, the opposing player will be reluctant to go forward so aggressively to defend against the ball carrier. The midfielder can then call for the ball to be passed to his feet (Fig. 2).

Section 3 - The Aims of the Game

The midfielder (6 or 8) gets into position to receive a pass from the central defender (3) or defensive midfielder (4).

The defensive midfielder (4) gets into position to receive a pass from the right or left back (2 or 5).

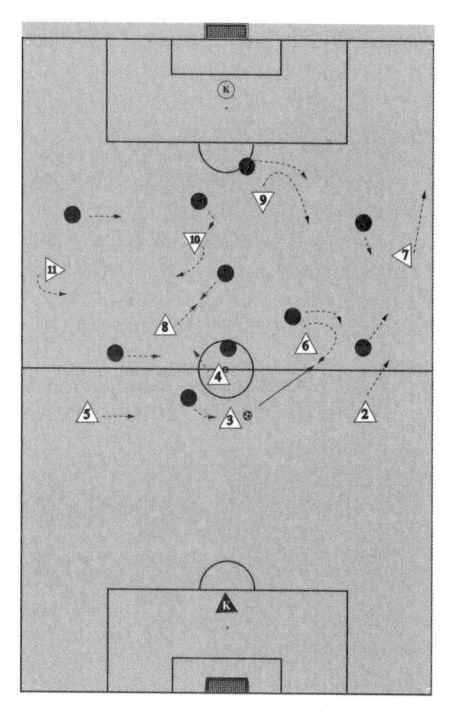

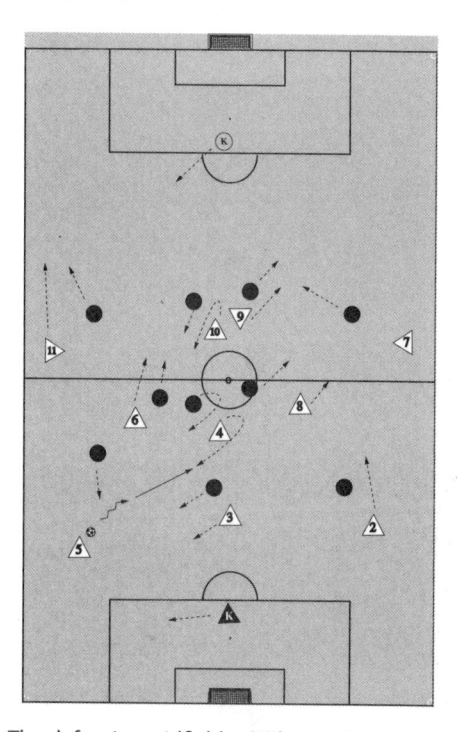

The right midfielder (6) makes a diagonal forward run and then checks back toward the ball.

The midfielder can create space for himself in 2 ways (see comments on passing to the midfielder from the full back position (2 or 5)).

- Run diagonally onto the ball.
- Run from behind the opposing player

The defensive midfielder (4) has an important function in switching the play from one flank to the other. When a full back (2 or 5) makes himself available to receive the ball, he must not run too far out of position. If he goes too far toward the sideline, the distance to the other side of the field is too great. His direct opponent will also move out toward the sideline. There will therefore be less space on this flank.

It is important that the defensive midfielder keeps as many options open as possible when he receives the ball. He can pass to a teammate on the same flank (11), or he can switch the play to the other flank. If he wants to switch the play, it is best to control the ball with the outside foot when he receives it. He will then be facing the correct direction of play and will have sufficient options open to him.

Book 1   Build-Up Play

When is the right moment to play the ball forward?
The right moment is when a defender closes in or puts pressure on the player with the ball. The forward pass cuts the defender out of the play.

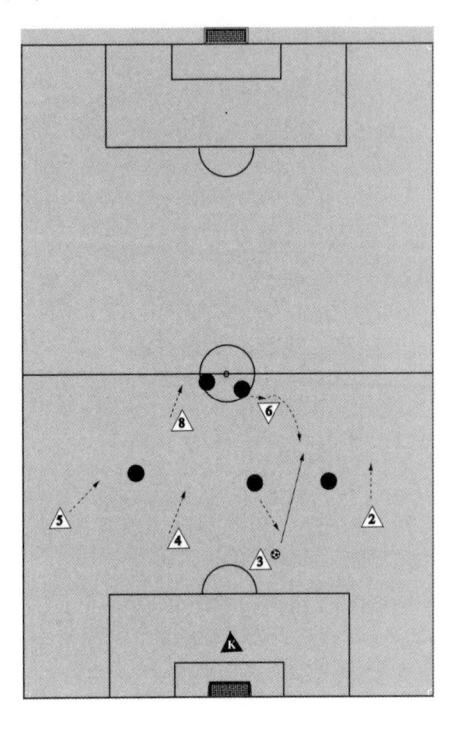

Build-up from defenders to defenders
If there are no options available for passing the ball forward, the ball can be passed to a defender. This requires great care to be taken. Simply circulating the ball aimlessly in the defensive line can often cause the defenders to lose concentration. Loss of possession in a team's own half often results in a scoring chance for the opposition or even a goal. Coaches of the youngest players must interpret "risk-free" build-up somewhat differently. Young players need to be able to experiment. Young defenders should not be discouraged from making runs with the ball and taking it past an opponent. Passing the ball to another defender is useful for switching the play to the other flank or passing the ball back. Passes from defender to defender can be regarded as part of the preparatory phase before the ball is passed to a player further upfield.

> "Many players need too long to control the ball!"
> *Aimé Antheunis*

Tips:
- Don't stand in line across the field. This makes defending easier.
- Stay focused, even when making or receiving a simple pass.
- Always communicate with your teammates.
- Pass the ball firmly. The faster the ball, the smaller the chance of an interception.
- Passing the ball square or back is the preparation for a forward pass.
- Try to be always available to receive a pass.
- Try to play the ball as far forward as possible.

Section 3 - The Aims of the Game

Cooperation between the central defender (3) and the defensive midfielder (4) in a 1-3-4-3 system

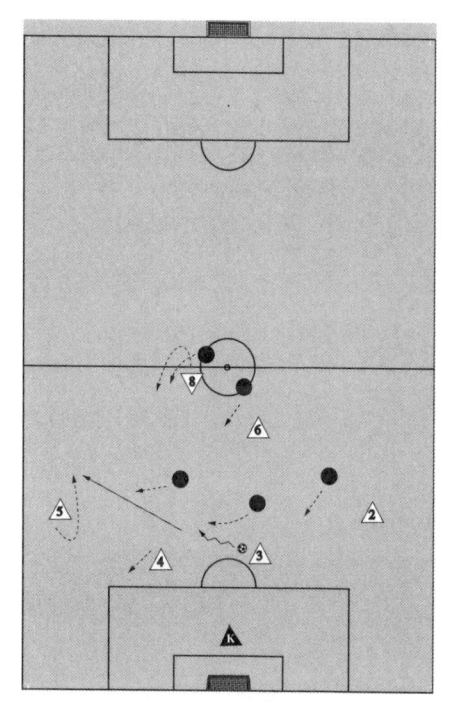

Cooperation between the central defender (3) and the left central defender (4) in a 1-4-3-3 system

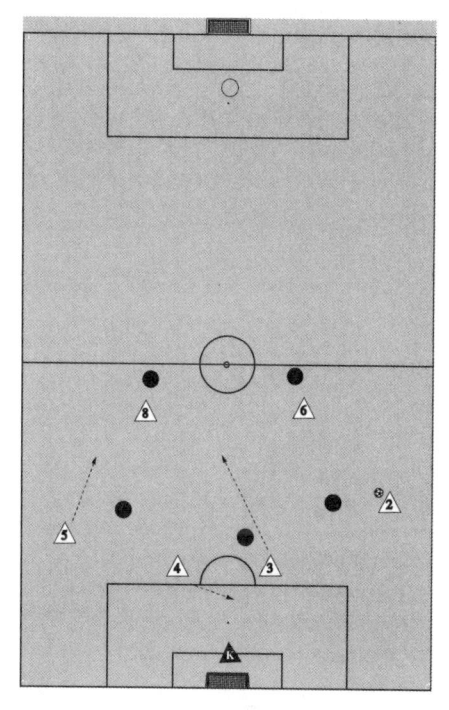

The defensive midfielder (4) has a pivotal role in the cooperation between these 2 players. The defensive midfielder is the support player and the extra man in midfield.

The ideal situation is when the central defender (3) and the defensive midfielder (4) regularly swap positions. In the example, the defensive midfielder (4) creates space by moving out to the left. He therefore has the space to push forward. He then falls back and takes over the position of the central defender (3). Swapping positions has the following advantages:
- The players learn the skills required in each position.
- Greater demands are made on the players.

There is a lot of talk about defenders pushing forward. But how many really do?

When the team is in possession, one of the two central defenders pushes forward into midfield.

In this system, too, one or the other central defender (3 or 4) pushes forward. This is more difficult for the opposing team to defend against.

When the right central defender (3) pushes forward, the left central defender (4) stays back.

Book 1   Build-Up Play

When the left central defender (4) pushes forward, the right central defender (3) stays back.

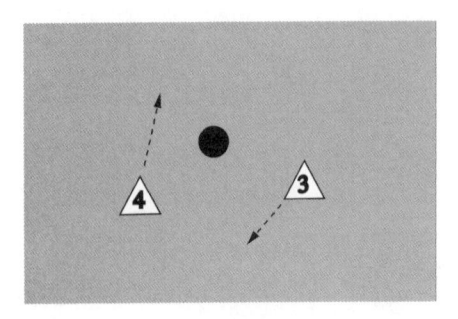

How can the defenders and midfielders increase the speed of their passing?

Playing a forward pass depends on various factors. Speed of action is needed to create an opening. If the ball is circulated rapidly, there will be moments when gaps open up in the opposing team's organization. At such moments the ball can be played forward. The following tips can help to speed up the ball circulation.

Missing out one player
Missing out the defensive midfielder (4).

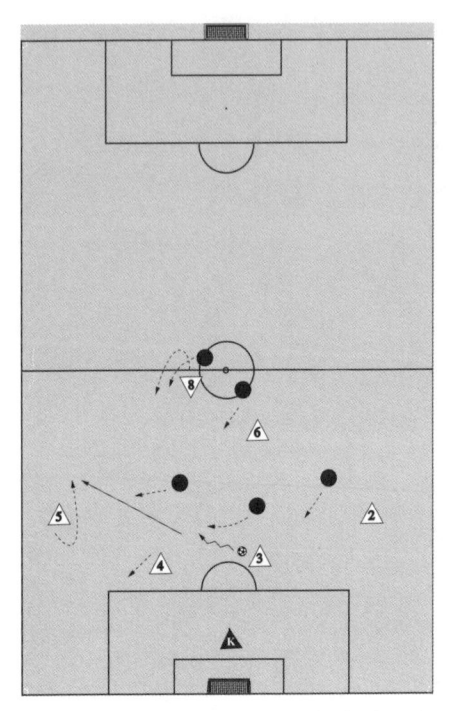

The goalkeeper has just played the ball to the central defender (3). The defensive midfielder (4) is level with him. Instead of playing the ball to the defensive midfielder, the central defender misses him out and plays the ball immediately to the left back (5). If he had passed to the defensive midfielder, valuable seconds would have been lost.

Section 3 - The Aims of the Game

Missing out the right or left midfielder (6 or 8)

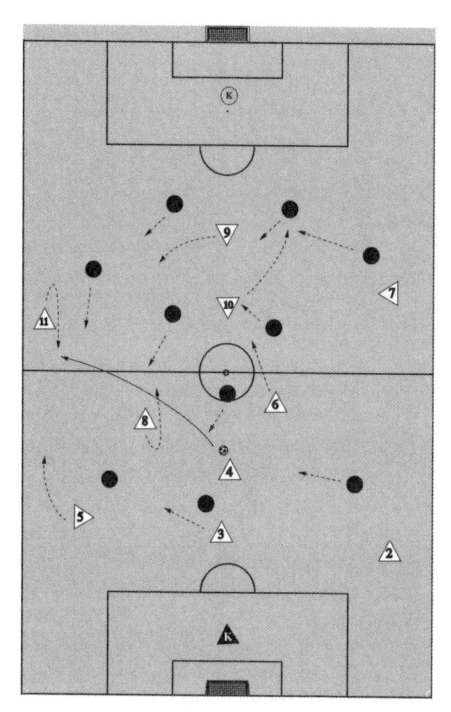

First-time passing
Passing to the flank

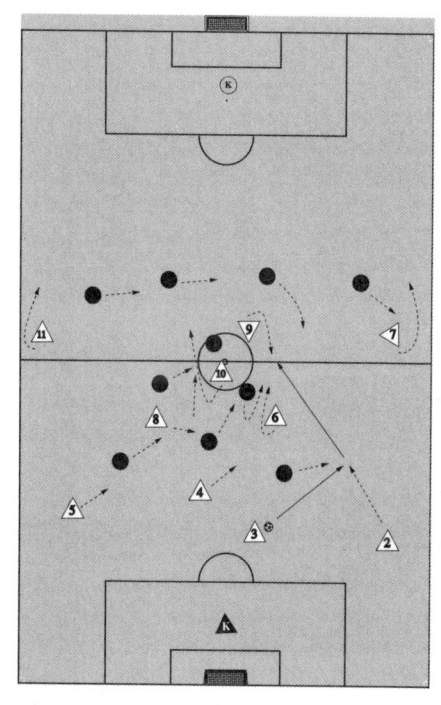

The defensive midfielder (4) has the ball. The left midfielder (8) has no direct opponent. However, the defensive midfielder (4) misses out the left midfielder (8) and plays the ball directly to the left winger (11).

A first-time pass can often be played. Young players often tend to play the ball from one foot to the other. A good example is the ball from the central defender (3) to the right or left back (2 or 5). If the ball is played into space in front of the full back, he can more easily pass the ball forward with his first touch. If the ball is played to his feet, he needs to control it with his first touch. The few seconds that are lost may be sufficient for the opposition to close down the opportunity of playing the ball forward.

39

Book 1 Build-Up Play

Playing the ball back into the center

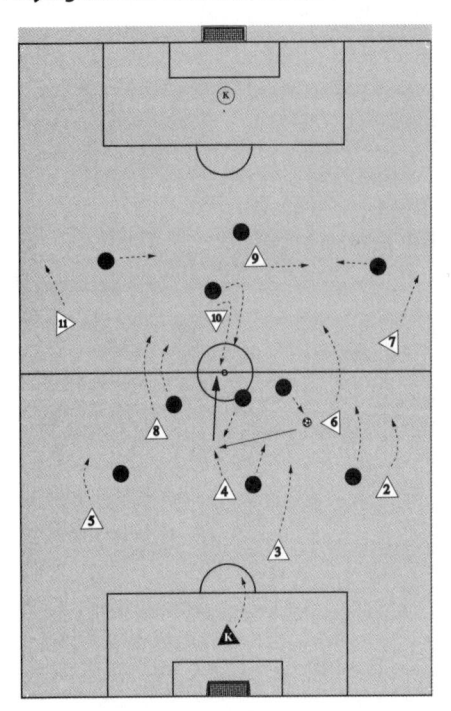

The right midfielder (6) has the ball and plays it back to the defensive midfielder (4). Instead of controlling it, he plays a first-time pass to the withdrawn striker (10).

What is important in this situation?
- The defensive midfielder (4) must size up the situation in front of him before he receives the ball.
- It must be possible to play the ball into the space in front of the defensive midfielder (4).
- The defensive midfielder (4) must play a firm pass.
- The withdrawn striker (10) must be alert.

Switching the play to the other flank

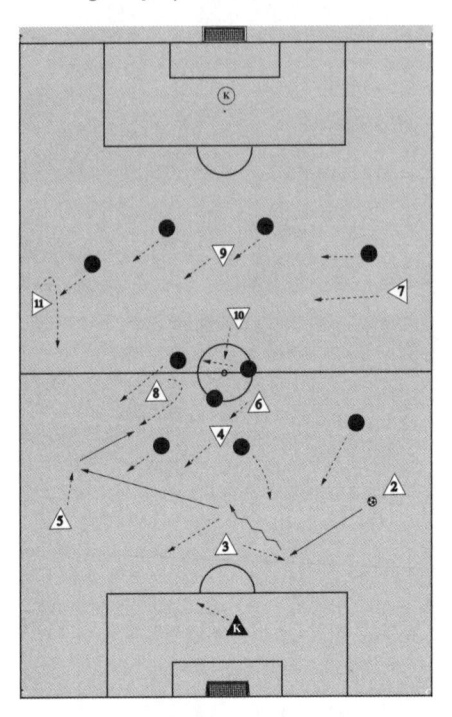

When play is switched to the other flank, it must be done quickly. The faster the ball reaches the other flank, the more time and space there is to act. If the switch can be made with one pass, this is the preferred option. In the example, the central defender (3) receives a pass from the flank. He has space in front of him, so he can take the ball forward and pass to the other flank. The left back (5) leaves sufficient space to advance into, so that he can play the ball forward with his first touch.

Section 3 - The Aims of the Game

Laying the ball off

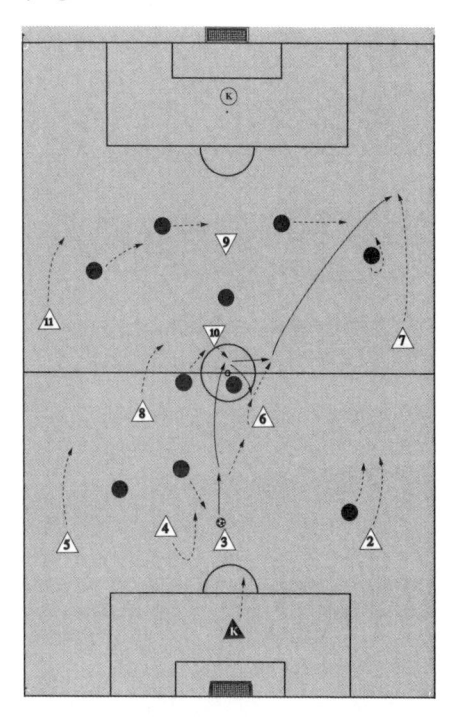

Communicating with the ball

A forward pass can often be played from a lay-off ball. The speed of execution depends on the players behind the ball. In this situation the defensive midfielder (4) plays the ball forward. The withdrawn striker lays it off to the right midfielder (6), who has made a forward run in support and plays a first-time forward pass to the right winger (7).

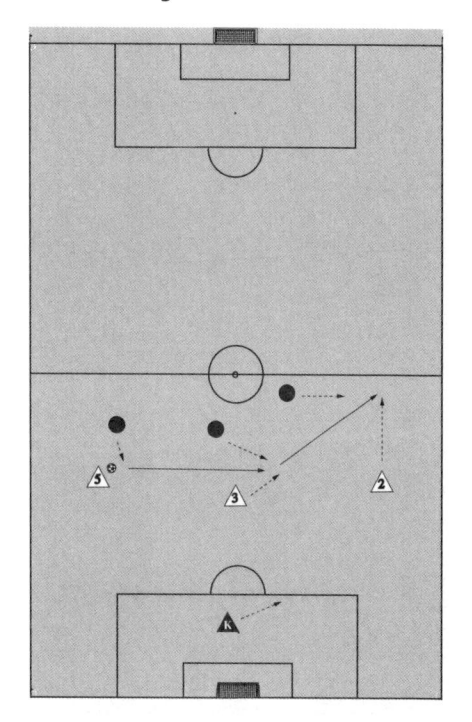

By "communicating with the ball," I mean that the manner in which the ball is played tells the receiver what he should do.

Examples:
By playing the ball in front of the central defender (3), who is in space with no opponent nearby, the left back (5) lets him know that he can turn with the ball toward the other flank.

Book 1   **Build- Up Play**

Passing to a player on the flank

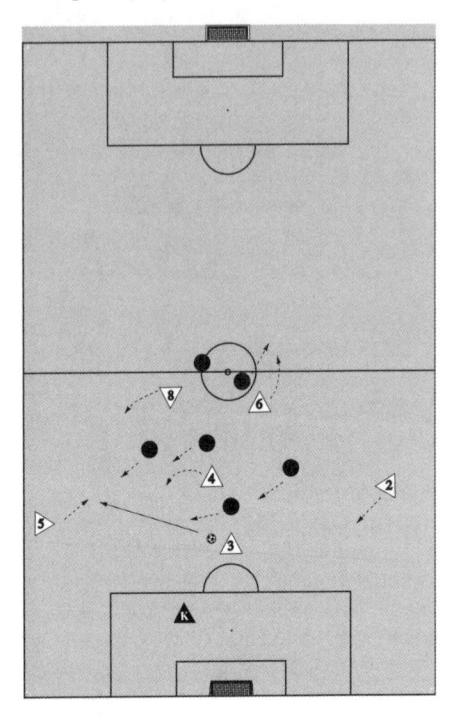

The midfielder (6) has a marker behind him on his right. The right back (2) plays the ball to the midfielder's left, so that the marker cannot get to it. At the same time the placing of the pass tells the midfielder he has space to his left.

Pace of the ball

Fast passing plays a major role in build-up play. Rapid ball circulation (depending on the situation) makes the opposing players cover a lot of ground in a short time. As a result, openings may be created. Fast ball circulation can be emphasized at all ages. From the age of 13 the players are physically more able to achieve this.

The central defender can play a rapid pass. The left back (5) is ready for the pass, which is directed to his feet. The faster he receives the ball, the faster he can act.

Section 3 - The Aims of the Game

Passing to a player in the attacking zone

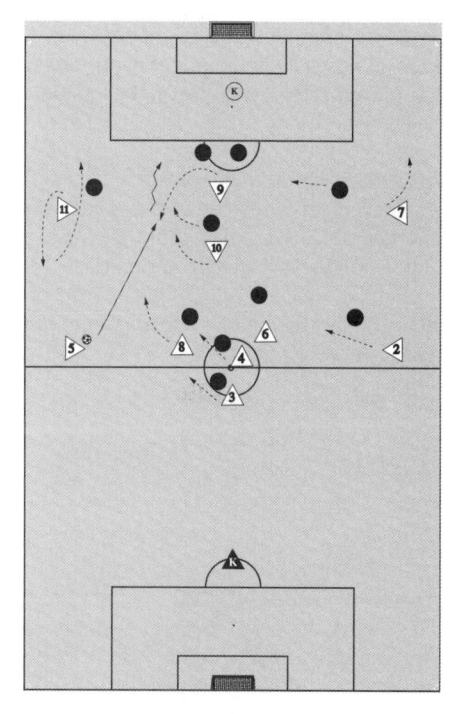

The striker (9) calls for the ball. His marker reacts too late. A fast pass gives the striker (9) more time to turn and go.

Key calls during build-up play	
Pass	Pass the ball
Free	There is no opponent nearby
Lay it back	Lay the ball back to the passer
Hold it	Keep the ball
Turn	Turn with the ball

Book 1   Build-Up Play

Build-up play against a team that plays a waiting game

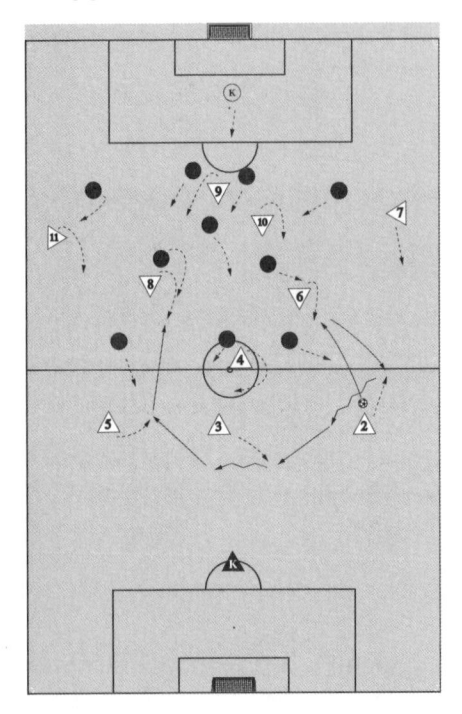

In youth soccer, we see more and more teams that play a waiting game. The coaches of such teams favor a close-knit system with lots of players behind the ball. They wait for the opposition to make a mistake so that they can mount a fast counterattack.

It is important to be patient when playing against such teams. The temptation to play the ball forward is often too great and this usually results in the team losing possession too quickly. The ball must be circulated longer to create an opening for a forward pass. It is a question of waiting for space to appear in the opposing defense, for example when opposing players advance to put pressure on the ball, and then immediately taking advantage of this to play the ball forward.

Requirements
- The defenders and midfielders must spread out more. This creates more space between the lines and therefore more opportunities.
- When the ball is circulated in the team's own half, there is a danger of loss of concentration. Concentration must be maintained, even against a limited number of opponents.
- The players must always be on the lookout for an opportunity to play the ball forward. The play must not deteriorate into an endless succession of square passes.
- The players must not lose patience and take unacceptable risks – this simply gives the opposition the chance to counterattack.

Build-up play against an opposing team that plays a pressing game

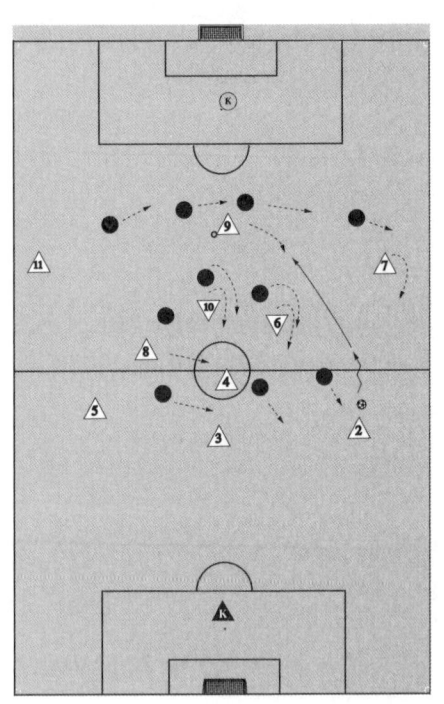

When the opposition exerts pressure on the ball, the players must take as few risks as possible. Pressure play can be countered by playing a long ball out of the zone where pressure is being exerted (e.g. from the right back (2) to the striker (9)).

Requirements
- Leave plenty of space between the midfielders and attackers (space to play the ball into).
- The midfielder (6) on the strong side (where

Section 3 - The Aims of the Game

the ball is) and the withdrawn striker (10) try to draw their markers toward the ball. This creates space between the midfield and attack, into which a long ball can be played.
- If the markers refuse to be drawn, the ball can be played to the feet of the midfielder or withdrawn striker.
- The striker (9) takes up position as far forward as possible between the right winger (7) and the center of the field. This makes it difficult for the second central defender to cover the central defender who is marking the striker,
- The right winger (7) tries to draw his marker toward the ball.
- The withdrawn striker (10) or the right and left midfielders (6 and 8) then move up quickly in support.

A second option is to switch flanks by circulating the ball quickly. This means that the opposing players have to cover greater distances to press the players in possession.

Defender receives the ball
When a defender receives the ball, he must be aware of the position of his opponent.

Some examples
Situation 1: The opponent is standing off the defender

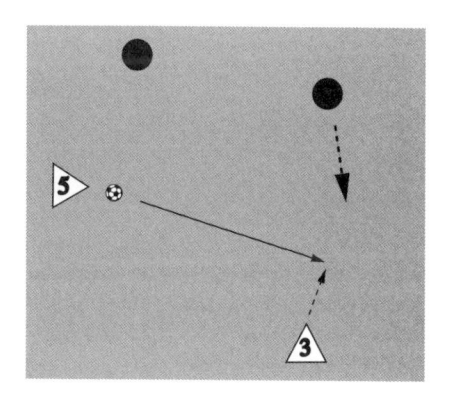

The defender has sufficient space to take the ball forward diagonally. He can then play it in any direction.

Situation 2: The opponent is close to the defender

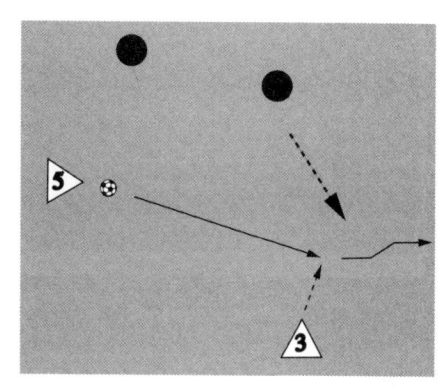

The defender plays the ball square after he receives it (away from the opponent). He can therefore easily take the ball in the other direction and has more time to pass it to a teammate.

Situation 3: The opponent puts pressure on the ball

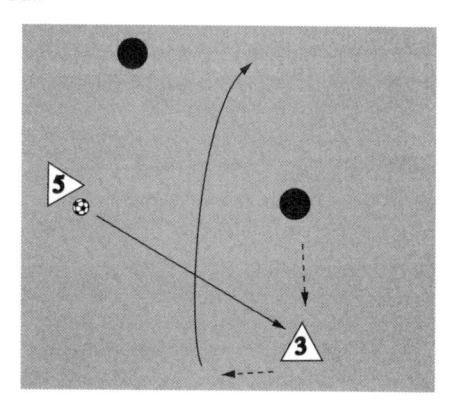

The opponent comes in to challenge for the ball. The defender cannot receive the ball and go forward with it. To avoid losing possession and win time to pass the ball, he plays it slightly behind him, follows it and clears it upfield.

Situation 4: There is no space
In some cases the risk of losing possession is too great and the defender simply has to clear the ball with his first touch.

Book 1 Build-Up Play

Section 4 - Coaching Ball Skills

Coaching ball skills

Book 1 Build-Up Play

Coaching ball skills

Besides the aims of the game, we also devote attention to the individual technique of young soccer players. I am convinced that the coaching of ball skills has a place in youth soccer. The coaching of the skills needed to deceive an opponent and take the ball past him brings added value to the learning process of young soccer players.

I view the coaching of ball skills as fundamental support. Most of the practice sessions will be devoted to match-related drills (with the obstacles and constraints encountered in real matches, such as opponents, teammates, time, space and a defined playing area). I base my treatment of technical skills on real matches. In practice a lot of attention is focused on fakes and dribbling tricks for attackers, with the emphasis on double scissors and stepovers. However, there are other skills in soccer. The ball skills applied in a real match are related to the aims of the game in a certain phase or in a certain part of the field. Build-up play, for example, requires different skills and movements than an attack in the opposition's penalty area. A build-up from the back is mainly about passing to a player in space and playing the ball forward. Ball skills are subordinated to these aims. Technique is a means for getting the ball into space and all that follows from this (circulating the ball to create opportunities to pass it forward). Risky fakes and dribbling tricks, which are suitable for an attack in the penalty area, are not suitable for use during build-up play. Build-up play requires skills such as the ability to turn away from an opponent, switch the play and getting the ball into space.

Section 4 - Coaching Ball Skills

The technical skills I deal with in this book are directly related to the aims of build-up play. I have chosen simple, effective and realistic skills that can help the players to get the ball into space. The most frequently occurring situations in build-up play are:
- Switching the play to the other flank.
- Opponent near you.
- Opponent behind you.
- Opponent in front of you.

"If you can control the ball, soccer becomes a simple game."

Ferenc Puskas

The aims of build-up play

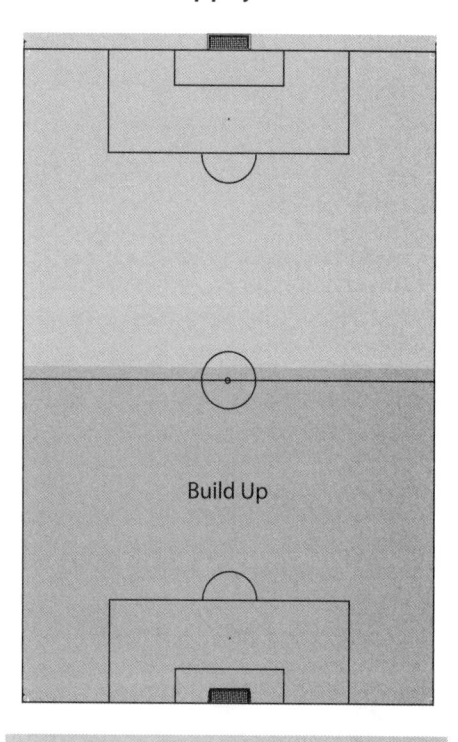

Aims:
- *To find a player in space by circulating the ball.*
- *To get the ball forward into the attacking zone as quickly as possible.*

Means:
- *Good positional play.*
- *Rapid ball circulation.*

Conclusion with regard to ball skills:
Technical ball skills support these aims.

Book 1 **Build- Up Play**

Switching the play to the other flank
The V movement
This movement can be used in the center of the field. The central defender (3) is challenged from one side by the opposing striker as he takes the ball forward. The defender drags the ball back and changes direction.

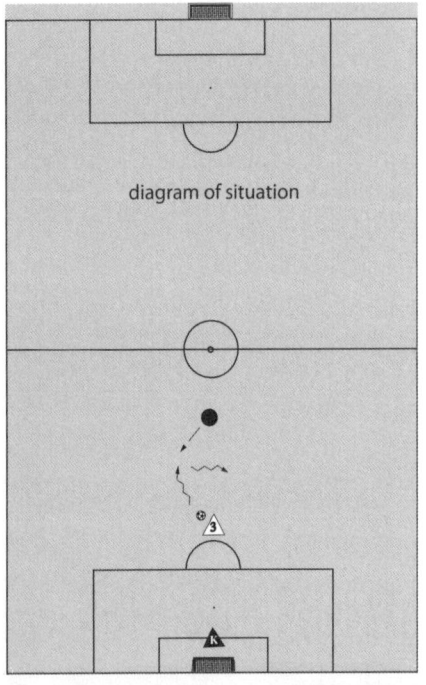

diagram of situation

photo of situation

Description of technique
Step 1: Place your foot on the ball.
Step 2: Drag the ball back under the sole of your foot.
Step 3: Push the ball in the other direction with the inside of the same foot.

Tips:
- If you make a short kicking movement with your right foot above the ball and also swing out your left arm, your opponent is more likely to be deceived.
- Change of rhythm after change of side.

Section 4 - Coaching Ball Skills

Stepover and allow the ball to run through

This can be used to switch play to the other flank. The ball is played from the flank to the defensive midfielder (4). An opposing player is positioned to one side. The player allows the ball to run though. He then turns and plays the ball to the other flank.

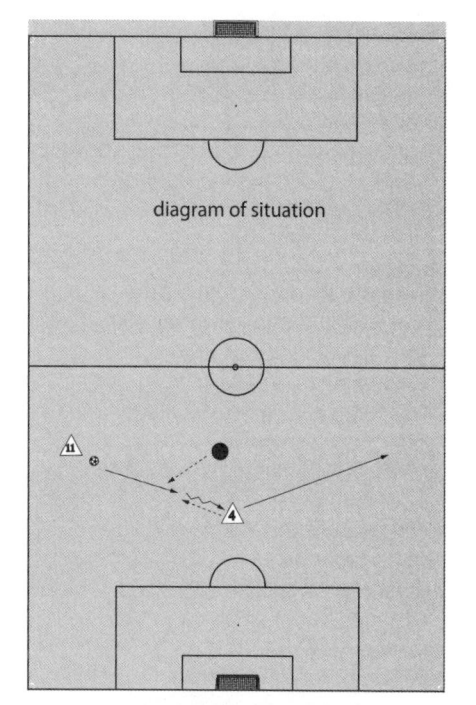

diagram of situation

photo of situation

Description of technique

Step 1: Step over the ball with your right foot from the outside inward and allow the ball to run between your feet.

Step 2: Turn quickly.

Tips:
- As you turn, make sure that the ball stays out of reach of the defender.
- If possible, cut across your opponent's path.

Book 1   **Build- Up Play**

Turn with the ball, using the inside of your foot

Same situation. The player turns as he takes the ball.

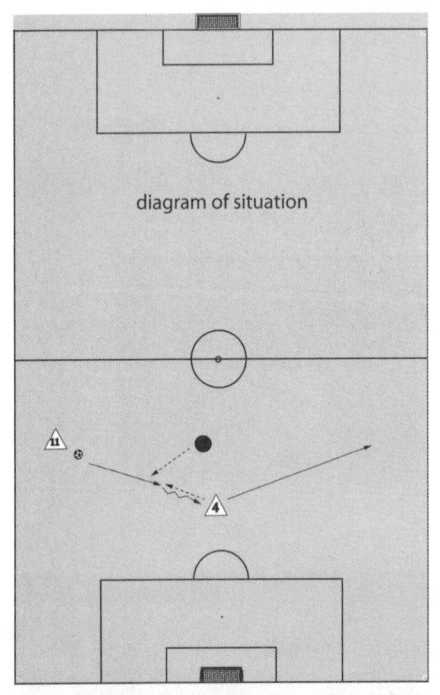

diagram of situation

photo of situation

Description of technique
Step 1: Place your left foot beside the ball and use the inside of your right foot to take the ball with you as you turn.
Step 2: Turn quickly.

Tips:
- As you turn, make sure that the ball stays out of reach of the defender.
- If possible, cut across your opponent's path.

52

Section 4 - Coaching Ball Skills

Opponent beside you
Stop the ball and turn back

The right back (2) runs with the ball down the flank. An opponent is near him. When the opponent moves to challenge him, the right back stops the ball with his right foot, turns back and takes the ball with him using the outside of the left foot.

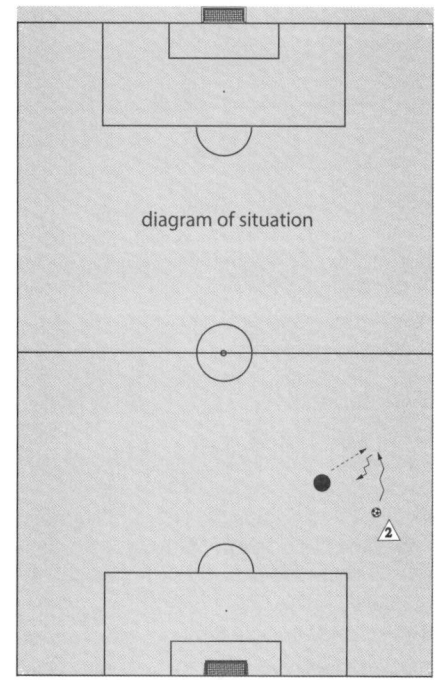

diagram of situation

photo of situation

Tips:
- Before the defender stops the ball, he can fake to cross the ball or play a forward pass (draw his foot back and extend his arm).
- If possible, cut across your opponent's path.
- Change of rhythm after turning back.

Description of technique
Step 1: Stop the ball with the sole of your right foot.
Step 2: Step over the ball with your right foot.
Step 3: Turn back and take the ball with you, using the outside of your left foot.

Book 1   Build-Up Play

The Cruyff trick
The midfielder (6) makes a forward run with ball at his feet. As his opponent challenges for the ball, the midfielder turns away.

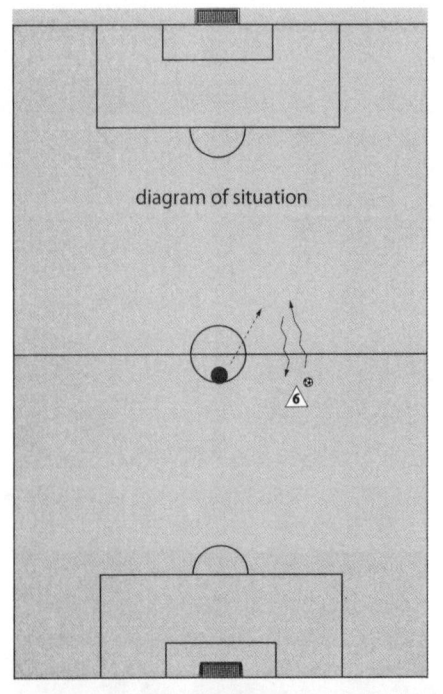

diagram of situation

photo of situation

Description of technique
Step 1: Place your left foot ahead and to the left of the ball, then use the inside of your right foot to push the ball across the back of your left foot.
Step 2: Turn and take the ball with you.

Tips:
- Position yourself as though you are going to kick the ball (draw your foot back, raise your arm).

Section 4 - Coaching Ball Skills

Turn back using the outside of your foot
The left back (5) makes a run infield with the ball at his feet. As his opponent challenges for the ball, the full back turns away with the ball,

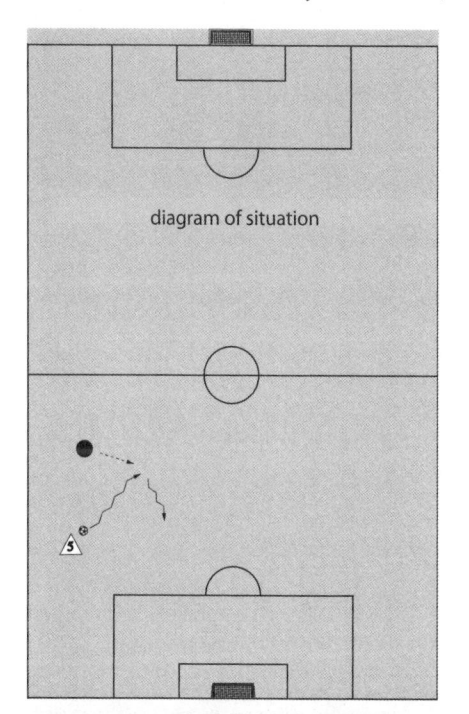

diagram of situation

Description of technique
Step 1: Keep your body between your opponent and the ball.
Step 2: Turn back with the ball, using the outside of your right foot.

photo of situation

Tips:
- Shield the ball with your body.

| Book 1 | Build-Up Play |

Stepover and turn back

The midfielder (8) makes a run with the ball at his feet. An opponent is on his left. As the opponent challenges for the ball, the midfielder turns away.

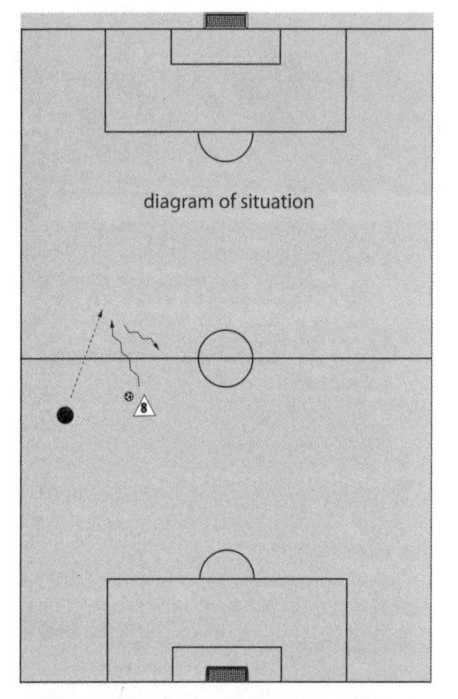

diagram of situation

photo of situation

Description of technique

Step 1: Place your left foot just ahead and to the left of the ball. Step over the ball with your right foot from outside to inside.

Step 2: Turn back and take the ball with you, using the inside of the left foot.

Tips:
- Make the stepover in the direction of your opponent.
- Quickly turn and take the ball in the other direction.

56

Section 4 - Coaching Ball Skills

Opponent behind you
Turn away from your opponent (using the inside of your foot; using the outside of your foot)

The central defender plays the ball to the midfielder. The midfielder has an opponent at his back. Depending on exactly where his opponent is, the midfielder turns away, using either the inside or the outside of his foot.

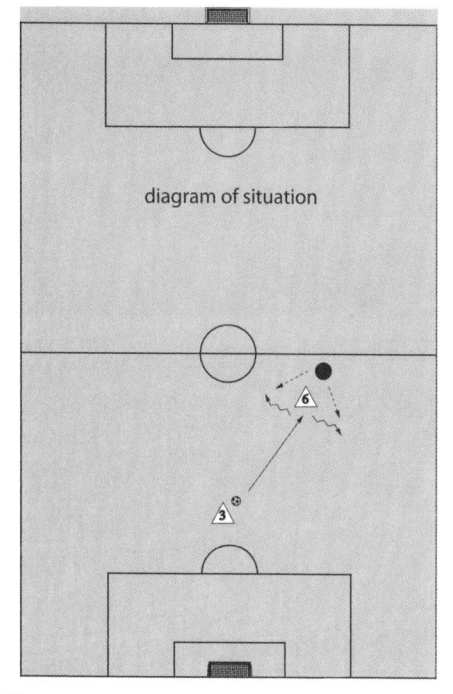

diagram of situation

Tips:
- Knees slightly bent.
- Screen the ball with your body.
- Change of rhythm after turning.

Turning away using the outside of your foot

Turning away using the inside of your foot

Description of technique
The opponent is behind and to the right of the midfielder. The midfielder senses this and turns away with the ball, using the outside of the left foot (Photo 1). The opponent is behind and to the left of the midfielder. The midfielder turns away with the ball, using the outside of the right foot (Photo 2). The midfielder can also use the inside of his right or left foot.

Book 1   Build-Up Play

Stepover and turn away from your opponent
The midfielder (8) runs to receive the ball. An opponent follows him. The midfielder steps over the ball to the left, turns and takes the ball to the right, using the inside of his left foot.

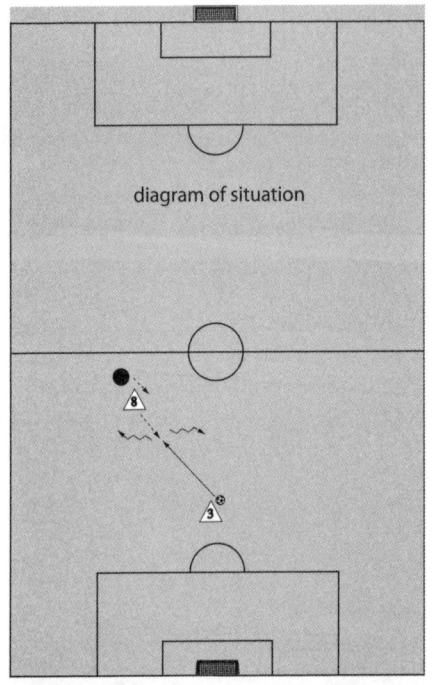

diagram of situation

photo of situation

Tips:
- Try to carry out the movement in one fluid sequence.

Description of technique
Step 1: Take the ball to right with your right foot and step over it from outside to inside, using your right foot.
Step 2: Turn away with the ball, using the inside of your left foot.

58

Section 4 - Coaching Ball Skills

Take the ball behind your standing leg
The midfielder (6) receives the ball in midfield. There is no opponent nearby. He pushes the ball across the back of his standing leg, turns and takes the ball with him.

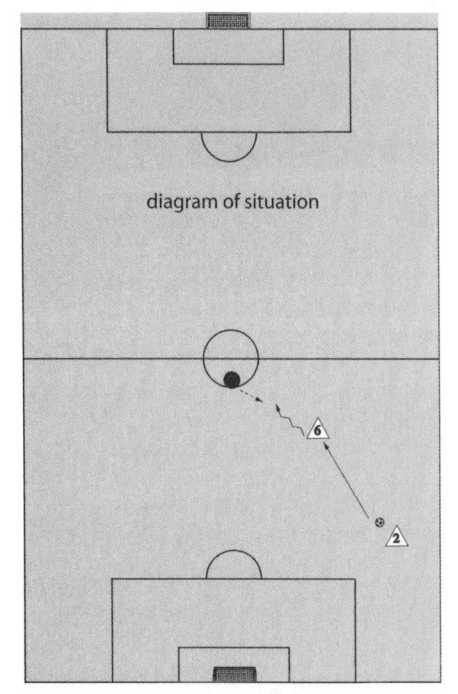

diagram of situation

photo of situation

Description of technique
Step 1: The midfielder takes a large step, placing his right foot ahead and to the right of the ball, and allows the ball to run between his feet.
Step 2: He then pushes the ball across the back of his right foot, using the inside of his left foot.
Step 3: He turns to his right and runs on with the ball.

59

Book 1 Build- Up Play

Opponent in front
Inside – outside

The midfielder receives the ball with an opponent behind him. He runs onto the ball at an angle to its path. He has sufficient space to turn and face his opponent. As the opponent challenges for the ball, the midfielder pushes the ball inside with the inside of his foot and immediately, without putting his foot to the ground, pushes the ball outward again with the outside of the same foot.

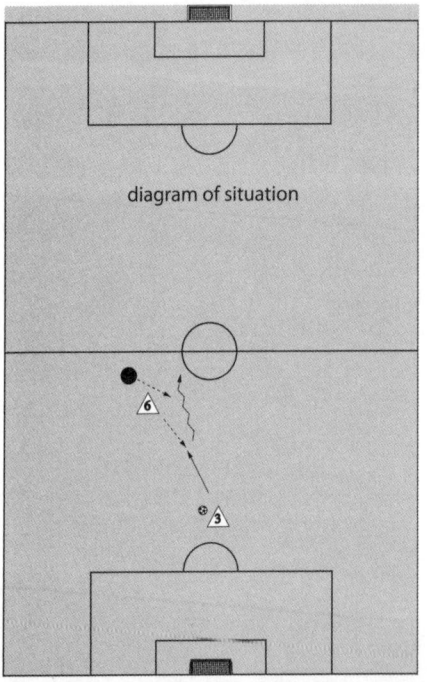

diagram of situation

photo of situation

Description of technique
Step 1: Your left leg is your standing leg.
Step 2: Push the ball inside (to the left) with the inside of your right foot.
Step 3: Immediately, without touching the ground with your right foot, push the ball in the other direction (back to the right) with the outside of your right foot.

Tips:
- Fake to go to the left.
- Knees slightly bent.

60

Section 4 - Coaching Ball Skills

Fake to kick the ball, then cut inside
The right back (2) makes a run with the ball toward the center line. He shapes up to pass the ball to the right winger (7) but then cuts inside, thus bypassing one opponent and creating more options.

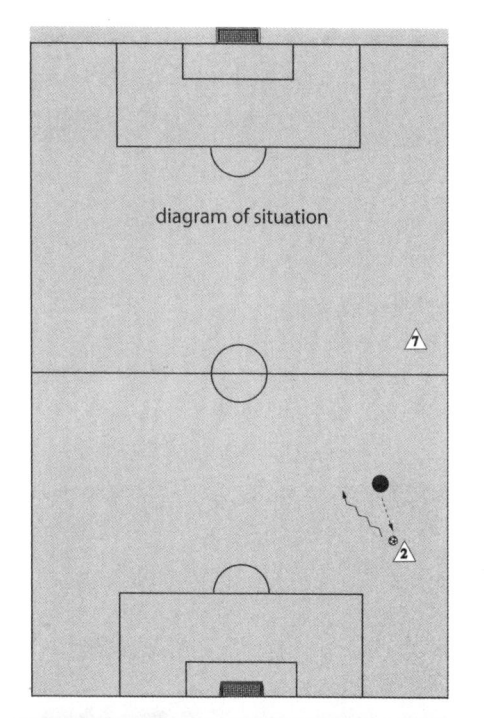

diagram of situation

photo of situation

Tips:
- The best moment to do this is when the opposing player is on the back foot.
- Cut across the path of your opponent if possible.
- Change rhythm after getting past your opponent.

Description of technique
Step 1: Run with the ball at your right foot and shape up to pass forward with your right foot.
Step 2: Drag the ball inside with your right foot and run with the ball, using either the inside of the left foot or the outside of the right foot.

Book 1   Build-Up Play

Various movements
Turning, using the inside of the foot
The winger plays the ball back to the left back. An opponent pressures the left back and he is forced to turn toward his own end line with the ball. He plays the ball with the inside of his right foot and turns infield. He then plays the ball to the central defender.

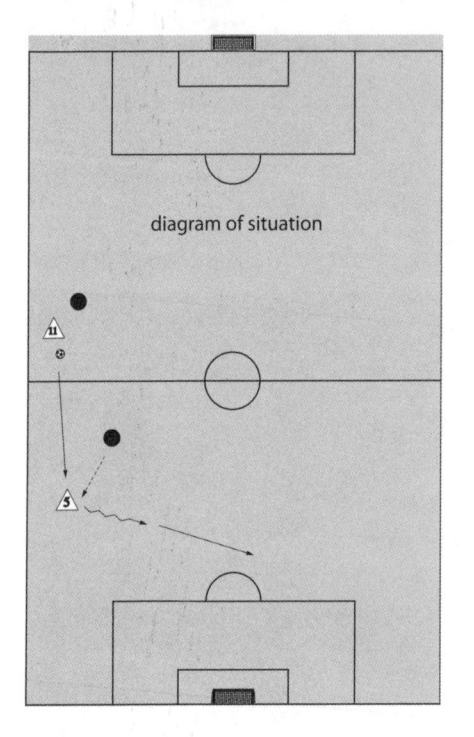

Description of technique
Step 1: Control the ball with your right foot and turn in one fluid movement.
Step 2: Allow the ball to run on.
Step 3: Change of rhythm with the ball.

diagram of situation

photo of situation

Tips:
- The ball can be played back with the right foot.
- Play the ball back as quickly as possible. Do not wait until your opponent is too close.

Section 4 - Coaching Ball Skills

HOW DO WE COACH BALL SKILLS?

There are 1001 ways to teach ball skills. In practice, all sorts of drills are used to stimulate the development of good technique. The drills that are chosen are not always productive. In many cases there is no clear relationship to real matches and the acquisition of ball skills is treated as an aim in itself.

Each drill has a given yield. The objective is to choose drills that enable techniques to be applied as quickly as possible in real soccer matches. In practice, this means that coaches ignore drills with a low yield. It is pointless to practice movements without an opponent when the players have outgrown this level. In devising a drill, a coach must take account of a number of influences. The content of the drill depends on these influences.

The objective is to apply the skills as quickly as possible in real soccer matches.

The level of skill of the players
Young soccer players who have already acquired some level of skill will be able to start functional drills or practice drills with opponents sooner.

Age group
The younger the players, the greater the emphasis on learning ball skills. Individual drills will be used. Older groups will carry out drills involving opponents.

Number of training sessions per week
The coach can focus more on technical skills if there are 3 sessions per week than if there is only one.

The coach's soccer background
In some cases the coach's soccer background plays a role. A coach who was a central defender will have a different approach to the technical skills of build-up play than a former winger.

The coach's skills
The coach's level of skill has a major influence on the coaching yield and the translation of ball skills into practice. It is impossible to lay down a fixed pattern for coaching technical skills. The practical situation determines the steps to be taken.

Requirements for coaching ball skills and the 1v1 situation

- *Ball skills and the 1v1 situation must be aligned to a position or a situation arising from a position.*
- *The coaching of ball skills must take account of the specific qualities of each individual player.*
- *Players must be encouraged to think about ball skills while learning how to improve them. Aspects such as when?, how? and where? are important.*
- *The place where the players practice the skill or 1v1 situation must bear a relationship to a real match situation.*
- *The players must play in the right direction.*
- *There must be a follow-up to the technical skill.*
- *The movement must be simple and efficient*

We have identified 5 steps in the translation of ball skills into real play. It is not the intention that the coach should go through these 5 phases. Depending on the needs of the group, the time available, the age of the players, and the coach's skills and background, the coach can choose from the following steps:

1. **Individual coaching**
2. **Functional coaching**
3. **1v1 with a "handicapped" defender**
4. **1v1**
5. **Translation of 1v1 into a match situation**

Book 1   Build-Up Play

Step 1: Individual coaching

In the requirements for coaching ball skills, we mainly refer to functional coaching of ball skills. In view of the faster yield, these drills are preferred. Individual encouragement of players is an option if there is sufficient coaching time available. The aim of individual drills is to practice the technical and coordinative aspects of ball skills. Since no opponents or match situations are involved, the players are not distracted but can focus completely on the movement. The movement can be repeated dozens of times. The movement becomes second nature.

> *The aim is for the player to be able to carry out the movement perfectly. Unnecessary obstacles (complex drills, run lines and situations) must be avoided.*

Unfortunately, individual coaching of ball skills is not always focused on technique alone. The drills are often too complex (difficult run lines and situations) and the techniques are not functional. The players are therefore occupied more with the organization, while the aim of the drill (practicing a technique or movement) fades into the background.

> *"The success of Ronaldo is the revenge of youth on modern soccer. With his adolescent solo runs, he thumbs his nose at adults with their heads full of serious deliberations about tactics and team formations. His phenomenal play forces coaches to fall back on 'Pass to Ronaldo!'"*
>
> *Auke Kok*

Individual drills must be as simple and realistic as possible. Simple drills with lots of repetition and functional movements take precedence. They are useful aids for learning how to reproduce skills faultlessly time after time. They can best be carried out at the start of a training session. When the coach sees that the players have mastered the techniques, he can switch to more functional drills.

Tips:
- Ensure that the techniques are efficient and realistic.
- Carry out the technique or movement step by step. Try to explain the technique or movement in stages.
- Ensure first of all that the technique or movement is carried out properly. The speed of execution can then be increased.
- The players should practice the skills on both sides of the field.
- Coach combinations of techniques or movements.
- Leave the players to themselves at first. Let them get on with it. Observe which players have which skills. Then try to broaden their range of skills.
- Do not try to do too much at once.
- It is fun to link a movement with a player's name, for example the "Steve trick."
- Try to encourage the players to practice their skills regularly. The start of the training session is the best time.
- Make sure that the number of repetitions is guaranteed.
- Choose simple organizational forms.
- Give the players homework.

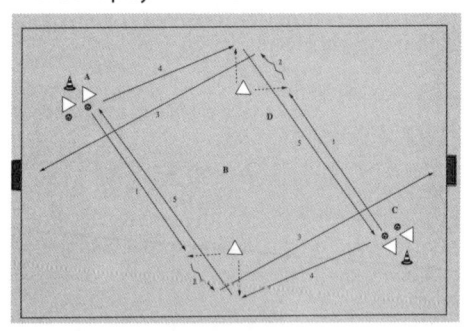

Examples of individual drills
We choose a drill in which the number of repetitions is guaranteed.

Switching flanks
The players practice the following movements:
- Receiving the ball, then the V movement.
- Stepover and allow the ball to run on.
- Turn using the inside of the foot.

Section 4 - Coaching Ball Skills

Organization
- 2 players in the center.
- Player A plays the ball in to player B, and player C plays the ball in to player D.
- Player B turns and scores in the small goal.
- Player D turns and scores in the small goal.
- Player A plays the ball in to player D, and player C plays the ball in to player B.
- Player D turns and plays the ball to player C.
- Player B turns and plays the ball to player A.
- Start again
…

The central players (B and D) score 5 times in the small goal. The players then change positions.

Opponent at your back
The players practice the following skills:
- Turning away from an opponent (with the inside of the foot, with the outside of the foot).
- Stepover and turn away from an opponent.
- Taking the ball behind the standing leg.

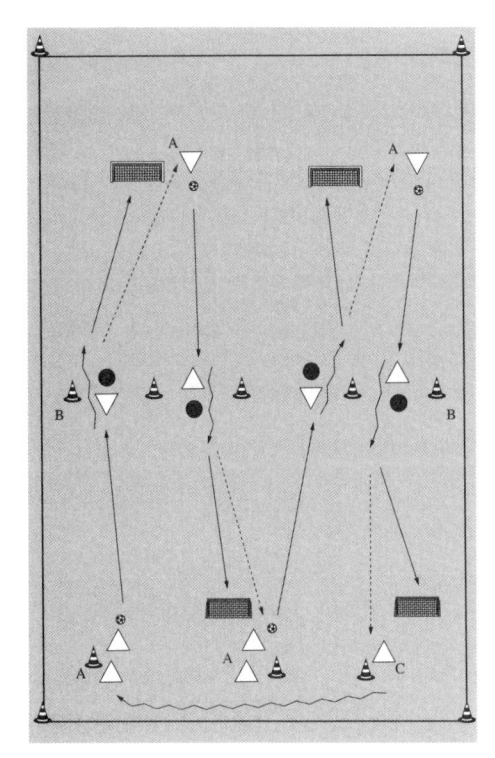

Organization
- Player A passes the ball through the cones to player B.
- Player B controls the ball, turns and scores in the small goal.
- The player in position C takes the ball from the following player to the starting point.
- Move to the next position: player A becomes the passive defender, the passive defender becomes player B, player B becomes player A, etc.

Opponent beside you
The players practice the following skills:
- Stopping the ball and turning back.
- Turning back with the outside of the foot.
- Stepover and turn away from an opponent.
- The Cruijff trick.

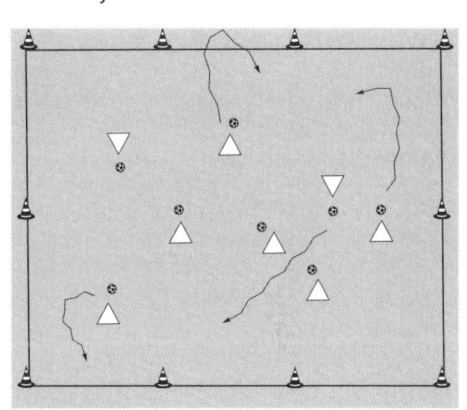

Organization:
- The players all run freely with the ball. When they find sufficient space between the cones, they turn with the ball.
- If they meet an opponent head-on, they can also turn with the ball.

Book 1   Build-Up Play

Step 2: Functional coaching

Functional coaching of ball skills is clearer for the players. The "recognizability factor" is greater. The location on the field, the direction of play and the situation are closer to real matches. The players grasp more quickly how movements can be used in real match situations.

Tips:
- See the tips for individual coaching.
- Ensure that the location on the field corresponds to the position in the field.
- Choose the right direction of play.
- Take account of the positions of the (virtual) defenders.
- Ensure that the technique or movement is executed with the right attitude.
- Ensure that the drill can be developed into a 1v1 situation.
- Ensure that the follow-up corresponds to the location on the field.
- The execution of the technique or movement must serve the aims of the game. Technical skills used in build-up play serve to 'get the ball into space'.

Examples of functional drills
Switching flanks

The players practice the following movements:
- Receiving the ball, then the V movement.
- Stepover and allow the ball to run on.
- Turn using the inside of the foot.

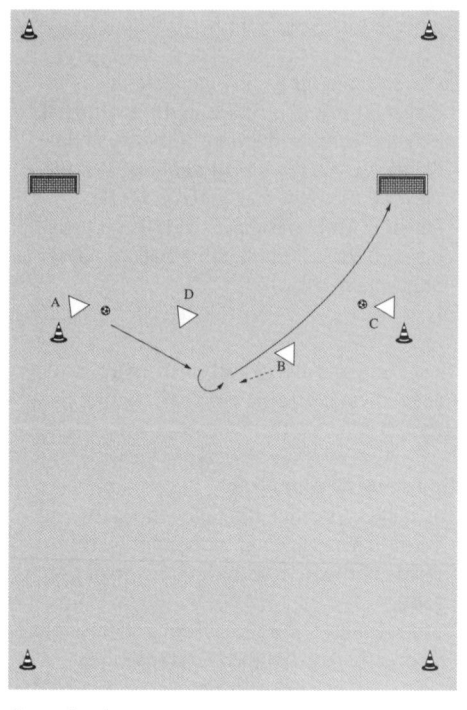

Organization:
- Player A plays the ball to player B.
- Player B turns (movement).
- Player B shoots at the empty goal.
- Player C plays the ball to player D.
- Player D turns (movement).
- Player D shoots at the empty goal.

Player A   = Position 5 or 11 (left back or outside left)
Player B/D = Position 4 (defensive midfielder)
Player C   = Position 2 or 7 (right back or outside right)

Coaching points

Player A/C
- Play the ball in firmly to the midfielder.
- Communicate: "Turn."

Player B/D
- Fake a lay-off to the passer and then turn quickly with the ball.
- Control the ball with your first touch.
- Don't let the ball roll past you.
- Shoot firmly at the goal.

Section 4 - Coaching Ball Skills

Functional drill with different movements
You can combine various skills in this drill.
- Movement with an opponent beside you.
- Movement before switching the play to the other flank.
- Movement with an opponent behind you.

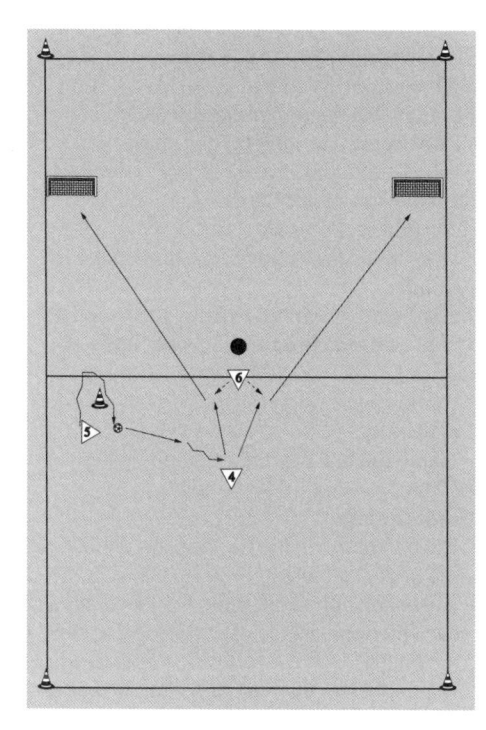

Organization:
Three movements are carried out in this drill.
- The left back (5) makes a forward run with the ball. He has no options for a forward pass and turns back with the ball (movement).
- He passes to the defensive midfielder (4), who turns with the ball (movement).
- He passes to the right midfielder (6).
- The right midfielder controls the ball and turns with it (movement) and then shoots at one of the goals.

The players then either stay in the same position (their own position) or move to the next position (follow the ball).

Coaching points:
The left back (5)
- Fake to run forward.
- Fake to pass the ball.
- Play the ball back with the inside of your right foot.
- Play the ball firmly.

The defensive midfielder (4)
- Don't stand too close to the defender.
- Try to control the ball and turn in one movement.
- Pass firmly to the midfielder.
- Play the ball to the defender's blind side.

The right midfielder (6)
- Use your body.
- Be aware of where your opponent is.
- First control the ball, then turn.
- Control the ball with your first touch.

Book 1   Build-Up Play

Step 3: 1v1 with a "handicapped" defender

A handicapped defender is a line defender, a zone defender or a defender with a disadvantage relative to his opponent (e.g. distance from his opponent). If the players can move directly from practicing a technique or movement to a 1v1 situation, this phase is unnecessary. A handicapped defender can always be introduced if the players are not very successful when they try out a newly acquired technique. Handicapping the defender gives the attacker a better chance of succeeding. A handicapped defender is especially useful when players are practicing fakes and dribbling tricks.

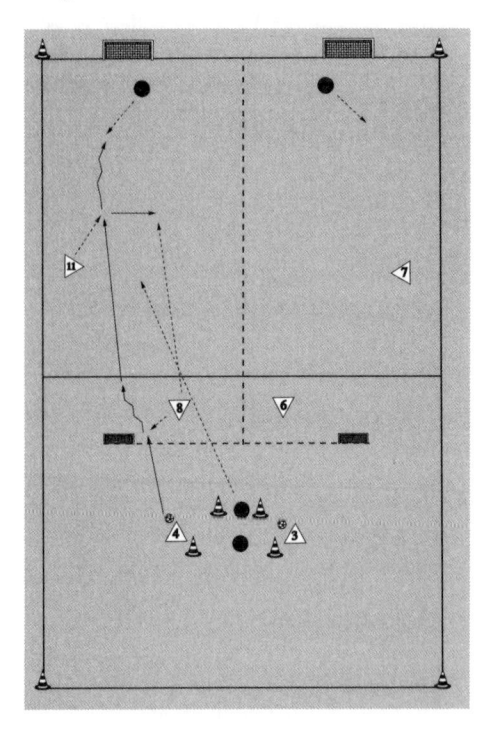

Tips:
- The resistance offered by the defender can be gradually increased.
- Ensure that the defender has a realistic chance of winning the ball.
- Ensure that the defender can score a goal if he wins the ball.
- The defender's position should be the same as his position in a real match.
- A handicapped defender can play in combination with a non-handicapped defender.
- Don't spend too long on this phase. Move on to 1v1 situations involving "real" defenders as soon as possible.

Examples of drills involving a handicapped defender

Turning with the ball in midfield
The players practice the following movements:
- Turning away using the inside or the outside of the foot.
- Taking the ball behind the standing leg.

Organization:
- The defensive midfielder (4) plays the ball to the midfielder who is in space (8).
- The handicapped defender first becomes active when the defensive midfielder passes the ball.
- The midfielder (8) must turn with the ball as quickly as possible.
- We then play 2v2.
- The attackers try to score in the large goal.
- The defenders try to score in the small goal.
- We then start on the other flank.

Coaching points

The player who passes to the midfielder
- Play the ball to the correct side.
- The more firmly you pass the ball, the faster the midfielder can turn.
- Keep the ball on the ground.
- Communicate with the midfielder.

The midfielder (6 and 8)
- Look over your shoulder.
- You don't have a defender behind you, so you don't need to check away.
- Turn quickly.
- Change of rhythm after turning.

Section 4 - Coaching Ball Skills

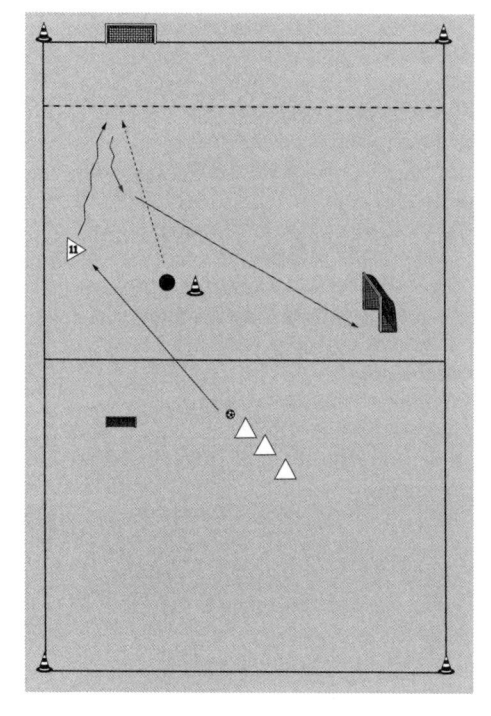

Opponent beside you:
The players practice the following movements:
- Controlling the ball and turning.
- Turning back with the outside of the foot.
- Stepping over the ball and turning back.
- The Cruyff trick.

Organization:
- The ball is passed to the player on the flank.
- When the ball arrives, the defender becomes active.
- The player on the flank can score a goal:
  - by running with the ball over the line and shooting into the goal in front of him;
  - by turning back and scoring in the goal in the center of the field.
- The defender can score in the small goal.

Coaching points:
- Go forward with conviction.
- When the defender reaches him, the attacker can:
  - slow down, keep possession and score in the goal in front of him;
  - fake to make a forward run, then suddenly turn back.

69

Book 1   Build-Up Play

Step 4: 1v1

Training for 1v1 situations is a core part of the acquisition of technical skills. When the functional aspects of ball skills have been learned, the 1v1 situation is the most important follow-up step. The aim must always be to bring out the relevance to real match situations. The direction of play, the location on the field and the relationship to a situation on the field can put a movement or technique into the right context. The coach must find situations that are suitable for making things clear to the players. The older the players, the more time can be devoted to 1v1.

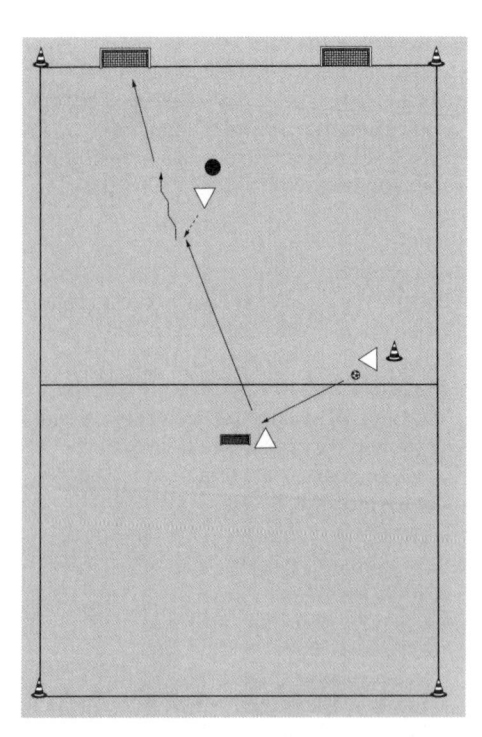

Tips:
- Try to work on the basis of a position or a situation associated with a position.
- Ensure that the opposition can also score.
- Ensure a good work/rest balance.
- Ensure that the location on the field corresponds to the location in a real match.
- Pay attention to the direction of the play.
- Encourage players to be themselves. Encourage the players to try out their skills.
- Ensure that the defender's position corresponds to his position in a real match.
- Build up to 2v1 and 2v2 if possible.
- Encourage the players; coach positively.
- If the attackers take the ball past the defenders too easily, the coach must encourage the defenders. The obstacles in the drills must correspond to obstacles encountered in real matches.

Examples of 1v1 drills:
With an opponent behind you
The players practice the following technical skills:
- Turning away from the opponent (inside of foot, outside of foot).
- Stepover and turn away from opponent.
- Taking the ball behind the standing leg.

Organization:
- The right back (2) plays the ball back to the central defender (3).
- The central defender (3) plays the ball to the midfielder (6 or 8).
- A 1v1 situation arises:
  - The attacker can score in one of the 2 small goals;
  - The defender can score in the handball goal.
- This drill can be built up to 2v1.

Coaching points:
The midfielder
- Attempts to escape from his opponent.
- Bends his knees slightly.
- Approaches the ball at an angle to its path.
- Senses where his opponent is.
- Turns away as quickly as possible.

Section 4 - Coaching Ball Skills

Switching flanks
The players practice the following movements:
- Receiving the ball, then the V movement.
- Stepover and allow the ball to run on.
- Turn using the inside of the foot.

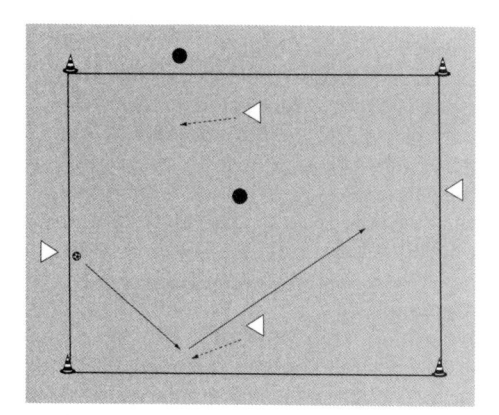

1v1 drills with different movements
You can combine different ball skills in this drill.
- Movements with an opponent beside you.
- Movements with an opponent in front of you.

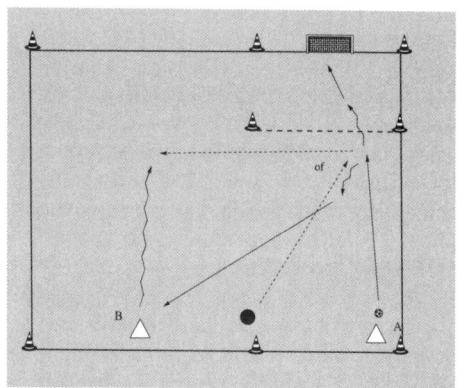

Organization:
In this drill we create a 1v1 situation:
- The 2 players in the square must not pass to each other; they can play a 1-2 or play the ball to the other flank.
- The lay-off players on the flanks cannot play the ball to each other.
- The lay-off player tries to pass to one of the central players.
- When the ball has been played to the other flank 4 times, another defender joins in.
- If the defender wins the ball, he must dribble it out of the square. The player who lost the ball then becomes a defender.

Tip: You can increase the level of difficulty by making the square smaller.

Coaching points:
- Fake to play a backpass.
- Turn as quickly as possible.
- Look where the defender is.
- Stand at an angle, ready to turn.

Organization:
- Player A tries to dribble the ball over the imaginary line; he can then score in the small goal.
- If the risk of losing the ball is too great, he can turn (movement) and pass the ball back to player B.
- Player B cannot join in until player A passes the ball.
- The defender must immediately move to defend against player B.
- Player B tries to dribble the ball over the imaginary line at the other end.
- The defender can score in both zones by dribbling the ball over the imaginary line.

Coaching points:
Player A
- Head for the goal with conviction.
- You can stop and then go on, or stop and play the ball back.
- You can fake to pass the ball.

Player B
- Sprint into space.
- Draw the defender.

Book 1 Build-Up Play

Step 5: Application of 1v1 skills in a match situation

The application of technical and 1v1 skills in match situations is often neglected. Unless they are used in match situations, however, they cannot be fully exploited. Placing technical skills in a match situation brings about a transfer of these skills

Technical skills can best be put into practice in small drills with lots of repetition. Drills such as 3v3, 4v4 and 5v5 are ideal for coupling the technical aspect to insight. The tactical aspects come more to the fore in drills involving more players (7v7, 8v8). In particular, the "where" and "when" aspects can be worked out.

The content of the drills need not always be oriented toward the skill. As indicated in the introduction, a skill is a means for achieving the aims of the game. The coach can offer advice about technical skills as appropriate moments during match-related drills.

Encouraging ball skills in match-related drills by means of:
- success moments
- tasks
- the organization of the drill

Practical examples:
Rewards
If a goal is scored after switching the play to the other flank, it counts double.

Task
The opponent is given the task of exerting pressure on one flank. The team in possession therefore has to:
- get the ball into space (movement);
- switch the play to the other flank.

Organization
We select a drill with 4 small goals. The players are therefore forced to switch the ball from flank to flank.

Tips:
- Avoid tasks that are too artificial
- Don't forget "free" play

General tips for coaching ball skills:
In coaching technical skills, it is best to start from the player's individual qualities. Each player has his own way of doing things. Let the players discover the drill, the skill or the situation for themselves at first. During this discovery phase (in which the players often freely practice the skill) the coach has the time to analyze the players' individual qualities. He can then take these into consideration as the training session proceeds.

Right attitude
When players practice a movement, they do not always do so with the right attitude. The drills are often carried out sluggishly, with little variation in pace. In the first phase it is important for the players to acquire the necessary coordination. It is pointless to ask them to speed up if they have not yet mastered the necessary technique.

When the players are in control of the ball, the intensity of the drill can be increased. This is the moment when the importance of a correct attitude should be emphasized. As their attitude changes and they become more determined, their technical skills come under more pressure. If the players carry out movements and techniques too sluggishly and with too little conviction, this will be reflected in match-related drills later.

- Increase the ball tempo – ensure that the (virtual) defender is put under pressure.
- Cultivate a winning mentality.
- Carry out movements with the necessary conviction.

Section 4 - Coaching Ball Skills

Ensure that the first touch is good
Ball control is often a major obstacle in a real match. Pressure can also be exerted in simulated competitive situations. You often see players set off on a run from a stationary position. This situation only rarely occurs in a real match. Confronting players with a variety of match-related passes (pass along the ground, pass through the air) forces them to develop their coordinative skills (receive with the first touch and go with the second touch).

- Make the players control the ball with their first touch.
- Touch the ball frequently as you run with it, so that you can react quickly if an opponent challenges.
- Try to control the ball with your first touch so that you can play it in the direction you want with your second touch.

Increase the tempo
Increasing the speed of the drills forces the players to react faster. This puts pressure on their skills and their speed of action gradually approaches that needed in a 1v1 situation. If the tempo decreases, this will also be reflected in 1v1 situations.

Tips for taking the ball past an opponent

Make a body swerve
- Keep your knees slightly bent (lower center of gravity).
- The body swerve comes mainly from the upper half of your body.
- It is very important to use your arms.

Time the body swerve or fake or trick properly
It is important to learn when to carry out a movement. Ideally this should be practiced against a real defender, but a cone or a line or a gate can also be used to help players estimate distances.
- Start the movement at the right moment.
- Take the initiative or wait for a reaction from the defender.

Accelerate after passing your opponent
The player's attitude is decisive here. If the player does not accelerate after dribbling the ball past a real or virtual defender, he is quickly back in the 1v1 situation. After passing a cone, there must be a change of pace.

What is the next step after going past an opponent?
Dribbling the ball past an opponent should not be an aim in itself. It must be done for a purpose. The player should know what he wants to do after leaving his opponent behind him.
- Be aware of the situation around you.
- Maintain your concentration after going past your opponent.
- Run with the ball, shoot at goal, pass to a teammate, cross the ball.

Book 1   Build-Up Play

Section 5 - Coaching Method

10-14 YEAR OLDS:
COACHING THE AIMS OF THE GAME

Book 1   Build-Up Play

10 to 14 age group

The players:
10 to 12-year-olds: The limited action radius of the young players has consequences for the play. The build-up often proceeds by means of short passes to the defenders and midfielders. In a game of 11v11, the players tend to maintain the same distance from each other that they have become accustomed to in games of 8v8. The distances between the players sometimes differ in relation to the size of the field.

13 and 14-year-olds: The players are physically stronger and therefore have more options in the build-up play. This physical development has some disadvantages. The players are less well coordinated as they go through a phase of rapid growth and their technique suffers accordingly. There is a greater tendency to opt for long passes.

Training sessions
Build-up play can be coached using drills with 1 line (positional training) or 2 lines. In the smaller drills, the focus is primarily on specific coaching points. Drills with 2 lines are used mainly to develop the players' insight. There is more emphasis on getting the ball forward. The session can end with a game of 8v8 or, occasionally, a game of 11v11.

10 to 12-year-olds: The coach can choose between positional training and drills with 2 lines. Passing and shooting drills are also an option, but build-up drills with real opponents are preferable because they yield more opportunities for learning. Passing and shooting can be used to emphasize the technical aspects of build-up play (receive, turn, pass).

13 and 14-year-olds: There is more emphasis on getting the ball forward. Drills with 2 lines, which stimulate the players' insight (6v6; 8v8), are ideal. More attention can also be given to switching the play from one flank to the other. The players are more capable of playing 11v11. They have a wider action radius and are more aware of the importance of getting the ball forward.

The coach
10 to 12-year-olds: The players in this age group are entering a new phase. They are confronted with new obstacles. The coach needs to give them challenges rather than impose tasks. By allowing the players a lot of freedom in how they play, the coach enables them to find their own path. A full back who dribbles past his opponent should not be criticized by the coach. The coach should instead point out other options, such as passing to a teammate.

13 and 14-year-olds: The players in this group can accept more responsibility for the effectiveness of the team and the build-up play. There is still room for individual development, but the guidelines for the build-up play are more strict. Defenders can be discouraged from dribbling the ball in their own penalty area. It is the task of the coach to point out other options.

The real match
10 to 12-year-olds: Under normal circumstances, build-up play is feasible. If the opposing team is stronger or exerts more forward pressure, build-up play becomes more difficult. The limited action radius of the players comes to the fore.

13 and 14-year-olds: The build-up play of the 14-year-olds in particular is smoother. The players have a wider action radius and more insight. They are better able to practice aspects such as build-up play and apply them in real matches. They can also adapt more easily to changing match situations.

Section 5 - Coaching Method

Aim

> The build-up module for 10 to 14-year-olds
> Aim: To learn 11v11
> "Learning to cope with match-related obstacles"
> Own position – 2 lines

Drills for the discovery phase

Passing and shooting drills

Positional training	Line training, 2 lines
2 : 1 =>	6 : 4 =>
2 : 2 =>	6 : 5 =>
3 : 2 =>	6 : 6 =>
3 : 2 =>	7 : 5 =>
3 : 3 =>	7 : 6 =>
4 : 2 =>	7 : 7 =>
4 : 3 =>	8 : 7 =>
4 : 4 =>	
5 : 4 =>	

Training phase

Line training, 2 lines	Positional training
6 : 4 =>	2 : 1 =>
6 : 5 =>	2 : 2 =>
6 : 6 =>	3 : 2 =>
7 : 5 =>	3 : 2 =>
7 : 6 =>	3 : 3 =>
7 : 7 =>	4 : 2 =>
8 : 7 =>	4 : 3 =>
	4 : 4 =>
	5 : 4 =>

Game phase

Match-related drill (8v8 or 11v11)

Book 1   Build-Up Play

The place of build-up play in a 10-0 defeat
When the opposition is too strong and the build-up play is of dubious value in terms of aiding the players' development, the coach has to find a middle way. A 10-0 loss is no indicator of the players' development, and indicates that the opportunities for learning when in possession were very limited. Continuously trying to build up the play from the back while regularly conceding goals is not very encouraging for the players. A good relationship between short and long passing can improve the situation.

Practical example: learning one of the aims of the game
Young players do not have much insight when they play 11v11. They need to develop further before they can play in a 1-3-4-3 formation. We therefore speak of learning one of the aims of the game in this age group. The players learn the principles of one of the aims of the game. The example here is intended for players who have not yet mastered the basic principles of build-up play.

We have chosen the following sequence for the players to learn one of the aims of the game.

We determine:
- The starting situation
- The age group
- The level
- The number of training sessions per week
- The starting level of the players
- The development objective
- What do we want to achieve?

We then choose the following steps:
1. What playing system are we going to choose?
2. Which module do we want to choose?
3. Which players are we looking at?
4. Which part of the field and in which direction?
5. What drills should we choose?
6. How should we factor in the age-typical aspects?
7. How should we draw up the schedule?
8. What should be the content of the training session?

We determine
The starting situation:

Age group: 11 and 12-year olds
Level: Regional amateur level
Number of training sessions per week: 2
Starting level of the players: The players have no "build-up background." They are not familiar with the principles of building up the play from the back.

The development objective:
- Build-up from the goalkeeper to the defenders
- Build-up from the defenders to the midfielders
- The backpass

1. What playing system are we going to choose?
The players in this age group play in a 1-3-4-3 formation.

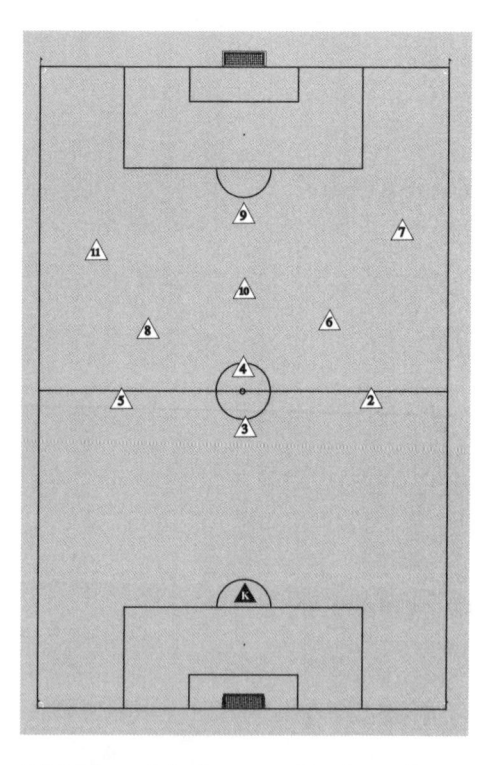

2. Which module do we want to choose?
The build-up module.

Section 5 - Coaching Method

3. Which players are we looking at?
Mainly the goalkeeper (1), the defenders (2, 3 and 5) and the defensive midfielder (4), in relation to the midfielders and attackers.

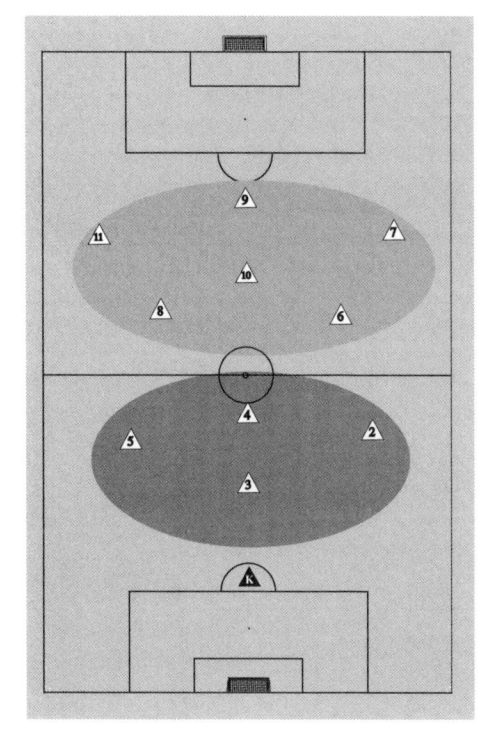

4. Which part of the field and in which direction?
In the players' own half, in the direction of the opposing team's goal.

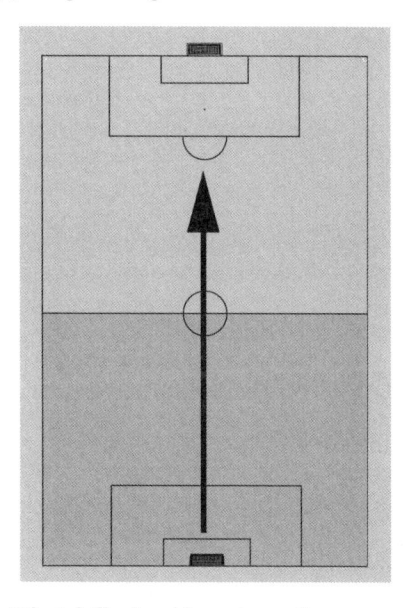

5. What drills should we choose?
- Passing and shooting drills.
- Positional training (from 2v1 to 5v5).
- Line training with 2 lines (from 5v5 to 8v8).

Passing and shooting drills are useful for focusing on technical aspects. Positional training and drills with 2 lines are eminently suitable for imparting insights into aspects of the build-up. The drills from 2v1 to 5v5 are ideal for emphasizing technique. Drills with 2 lines are again more about insight. The aim is to combine the two.

6. How should we factor in the age-typical aspects?
The 10 to 14 age group is in the learning phase for 11v11. Besides developing general skills, it is important to put the players more or less in their own positions. There is no point in putting attackers in build-up positions to practice build-up play. The players need all their time to familiarize themselves with all the development aspects associated with their own positions.

Book 1   Build-Up Play

7. How should we draw up the schedule?
This schedule is simply an example. Coaches should not simply copy it. Factors such as enthusiasm, form on the day, the translation of the aim of the game in practice and the time of year all influence the scheduling of the training sessions. Coaches must translate the aim of the game into practice in ways that suit their own situation.

Tuesday	**training**	**tactical**	**build-up**	**session 1**
Thursday	**training**	**tactical**	**build-up**	**session 2**
Saturday	match			
Tuesday	training	technical	changing direction and turning/positional play/match-related drill	
Thursday	**training**	**tactical**	**build-up**	**session 3**
Saturday	match			
Tuesday	training	tournament drill (4v4)		
Thursday	**training**	**tactical**	**build-up**	**session 4**
Saturday	match			
Tuesday	training	technical	passing, receiving and finishing/positional play/match-related drill	
Thursday	training	finishing drills	match-related drill	
Saturday	match			
Tuesday	**training**	**tactical**	**build-up**	**session 5**
Thursday	**training**	**tactical**	**build-up**	**session 6**
Saturday	match			

Section 5 - Coaching Method

8. What should be the content of the training session?
The development objectives of the sessions.

In **session 1** we start with a simple passing and shooting drill. Simple because, in the first phase, we are only concerned with the content, i.e. a defender receives the ball in the penalty area. In the training phase we then switch to a drill with a limited number of teammates and opponents. This enables technique to be combined more easily with insight. We end the session with a match-related drill with a success moment for the players.

In **session 2** the passing and shooting drill is made more difficult. After a cross, the players have to exploit a 2v1 situation and then pass to the striker. The positional training is also taken further. Two full backs are introduced. The same success moment is included in the match-related drill.

Session 3 goes back one step further. The passing and shooting drill is replaced by a drill in which the attacker also faces an opponent. In the training phase we go further with the positional drill from the previous session. If the players are good enough, another opponent is introduced. We end the session with a match-related drill (free play).

From **session 4** we introduce a positional game in the discovery phase, in which receiving the ball, taking up positions to receive the ball, etc. are central. This drill is very technical. The players have already experienced 3 sessions with smaller drills (positional training). It is now time for a drill with 2 lines (6 + goalkeeper v 4). Match-related drill with free play.

Session 5 builds on the previous sessions. The organization of the passing and shooting drill is modified slightly (with 4 goals). The line drill is developed further in the training phase.

In **session 6**, the level of difficulty in the drills is increased. The session finishes with a traditional match-related drill.

Book 1 Build-Up Play

Session 1
Development objective of the session
In session 1 we start with a simple passing and shooting drill. Simple because, in the first phase, we are only concerned with the content, i.e. a defender receives the ball in the penalty area. In the training phase we then switch to a drill with a limited number of teammates and opponents. This enables technique to be combined more easily with insight. We end the session with a match-related drill with a success moment for the players.

Discovery phase: Passing and shooting drill
Training phase: Positional training (3 + goalkeeper v 2)
Game phase: Match-related drill (8v8, depending on the number of available players)

Content of the session
Discovery phase:
Passing and shooting drill

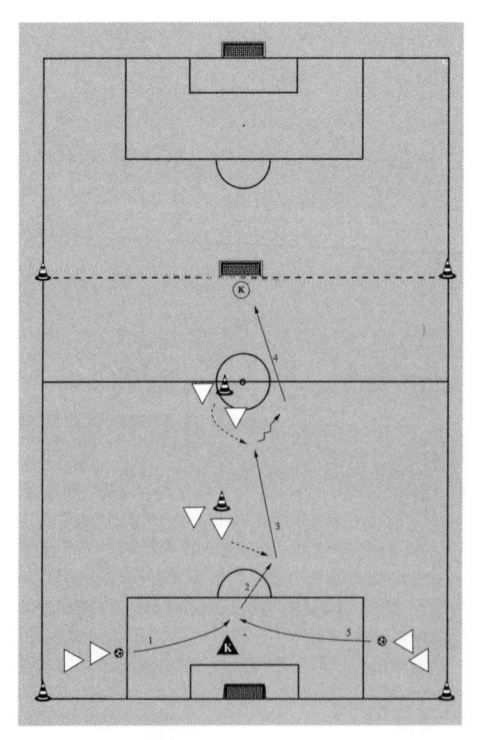

Organization:
- Cross to the goalkeeper (distance depends on the level of the players)
- The goalkeeper plays the ball diagonally to the defender.
- The defender controls the ball and plays it forward to the advanced striker.
- The striker controls the ball, turns and shoots at goal.

The sequence is then repeated, starting with a cross from the other flank. The central defender calls for the ball on the other side.

The players move up one position by following the ball.

Coaching points:
- Stay out of the penalty area.
- Use the outside foot to receive the ball.
- Stand at an angle to the path of the ball to receive it.
- Control the ball with your first touch and pass it with your second touch.
- Play the ball firmly to the striker.

Section 5 - Coaching Method

Training phase: Positional training (3 + goalkeeper v 2)

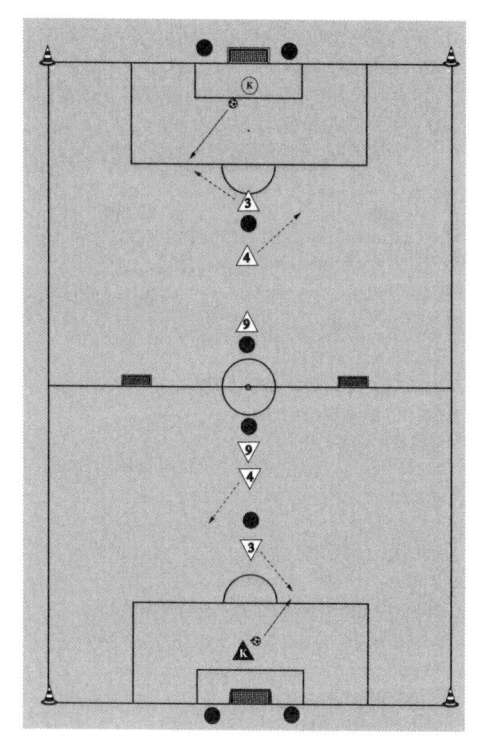

Organization:
- We play 3 + goalkeeper v 2.
- The team of 3 scores in one of the 2 small goals.
- The team of 2 scores in the large goal.

A new team of 2 replaces the first one if the team of 3 scores.

Coaching points:
- Stay far enough apart.
- Stand at an angle to the path of the ball to receive it.
- Look for the most advanced striker.
- Support each other.

Success moment
Who is the first to score 5 goals?

Game phase:
8v8, depending on the number of available players
Success moment: Each goal resulting from a build-up by the goalkeeper or defenders without losing possession counts double.

Book 1   Build-Up Play

Session 2
Development objective of the session
In session 2 the passing and shooting drill is made more difficult. After a cross, the players have to exploit a 2v1 situation and then pass to the striker. The positional training is also taken further. Two full backs are introduced. The same success moment is included in the match-related drill.

Discovery phase: Passing and shooting drill with 2v1 situation
Training phase: Positional training (5 + goalkeeper v 3)
Game phase: Match-related drill (8v8, depending on the number of available players)

Content of the session
Discovery phase: Passing and shooting drill with 2v1 situation

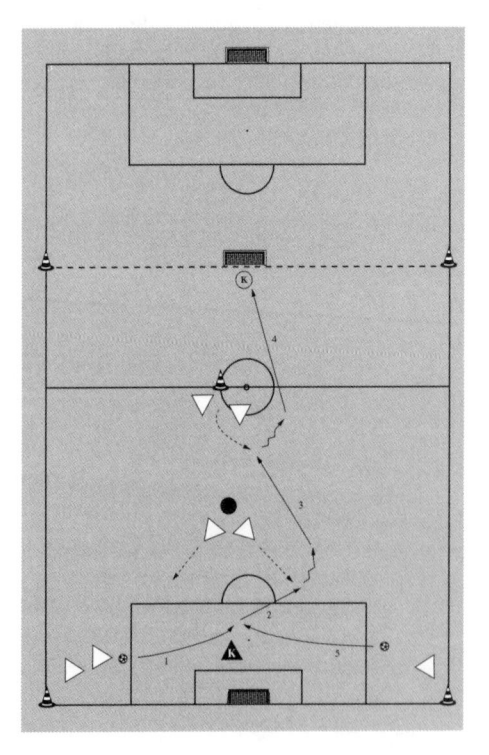

Organization:
- Cross to the goalkeeper (distance depends on the level of the players)
- The goalkeeper plays the ball to one of the defenders.
- The defender controls the ball and plays it forward to the advanced striker.
- The striker controls the ball, turns and shoots at goal.

The sequence is then repeated, starting with a cross from the other flank. If the opponent between the two defenders wins the ball he can score in the large goal.

Moving to the next position:
The player who crosses takes over from one of the central defenders.
The defender who plays the ball forward to the striker takes over from the striker.

Coaching points:
- Stay out of the penalty area.
- Use the outside foot to receive the ball.
- Stand at an angle to the path of the ball to receive it.
- Control the ball with your first touch and pass it with your second touch.
- Try to play the ball forward when the defender challenges.
- Play the ball firmly to the striker.

Section 5 - Coaching Method

Training phase: Positional training (5 + K v 3 - 4)

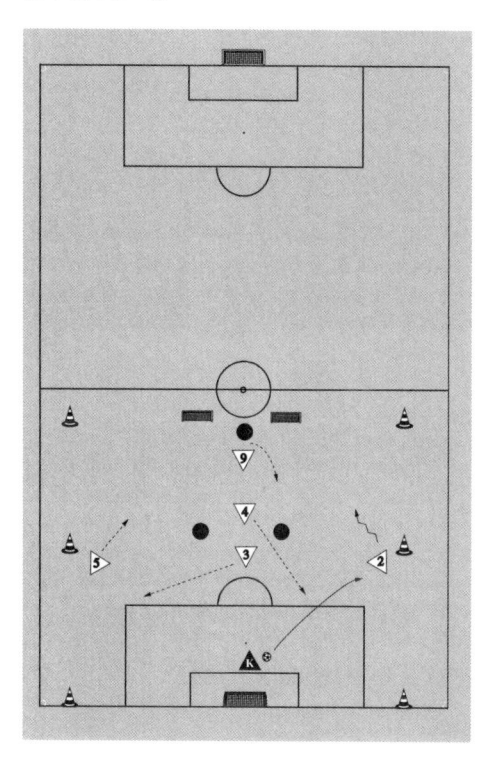

Organization:
- We play 5 + goalkeeper v 3.
- The team of 5 tries to outplay the team of 3 and score in the small goals.
- The team of 3 can score in the large goal.

Coaching points:
All Players
- Try to get the ball to the free player.
- Try to get the ball forward as quickly as possible.
- Support each other.

Central defenders
- Stand far enough apart
- Stand at an angle to the path of the ball to receive it.

Full backs
- Stand as far forward as possible.
- Make yourself available.

Game phase:
8v8, depending on the number of available players.
Free play.

Book 1 Build- Up Play

Session 3
Development objective of the session
Session 3 goes back one step further. The passing and shooting drill is replaced by a drill in which the attacker also faces an opponent. In the training phase we go further with the positional drill from the previous session. If the players are good enough, another opponent is introduced. We end the session with a match-related drill (free play).

Discovery phase: Positional training (3 + goalkeeper v 2 + goalkeeper situation)
Training phase: Positional training (5 + goalkeeper v 3 - 4)
Game phase: Match-related drill (8v8, depending on the number of available players)

Content of the session
Discovery phase: Positional training (3 + K v 2 + K situation)

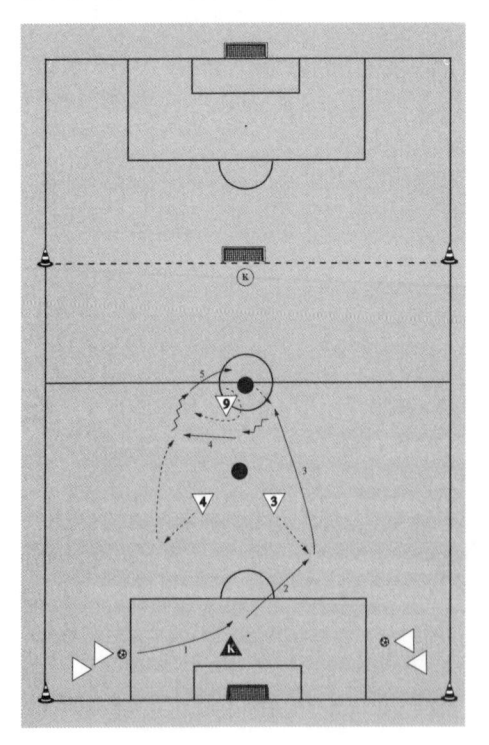

Organization:
- Cross to the goalkeeper (distance depends on the level of the players)
- The goalkeeper plays the ball to one of the defenders.
- The defender controls the ball. Then play 3 + goalkeeper v 2 + goalkeeper.
- After a goal is scored, we start from the other side. A time limit can also be set.

Moving to the next position:
The player who crosses takes over from one of the central defenders. The defender who plays the ball forward to the striker takes over from the striker.

Coaching points:
- Stay out of the penalty area.
- Use the outside foot to receive the ball.
- Stand at an angle to the path of the ball to receive it.
- Control the ball with your first touch and pass it with your second touch.
- Try to play the ball forward when the defender challenges.
- Play the ball firmly to the striker.

Success moment:
The team of two is winning 1-0. Who is the first to score 5 goals?

Section 5 - Coaching Method

Training phase: Positional training (5 + goalkeeper v 3)

Organization:
- We play 5 + goalkeeper v 3.
- The team of 5 tries to outplay the team of 3.
- The team of 5 can score in the small goals.
- The team of 3 can score in the large goal.

Coaching points:
All Players
- Try to get the ball to the free player.
- Try to get the ball forward as quickly as possible.
- Support each other.

Central defenders
- Stand far enough apart
- Stand at an angle to the path of the ball to receive it.

Full backs
Stand as far forward as possible.

Game phase:
8v8, depending on the number of available players
Success moment: Each goal resulting from a build-up by the goalkeeper or defenders without losing possession counts double.

87

Book 1   Build-Up Play

Session 4
Development objective of the session
From session 4 we introduce a positional game in the discovery phase, in which receiving the ball, taking up positions to receive the ball, etc. are central. This drill is very technical. The players have already experienced 3 sessions with smaller drills (positional training). It is now time for a drill with 2 lines (6 + goalkeeper v 4). Match-related drill with free play.

Discovery phase: Positional play (5 v 2/3)
Training phase: Line training with 2 lines (6 + goalkeeper v 4)
Game phase: Match-related drill (8v8, depending on the number of available players)

Content of the session
Discovery phase: Positional play (5 v 2/3)

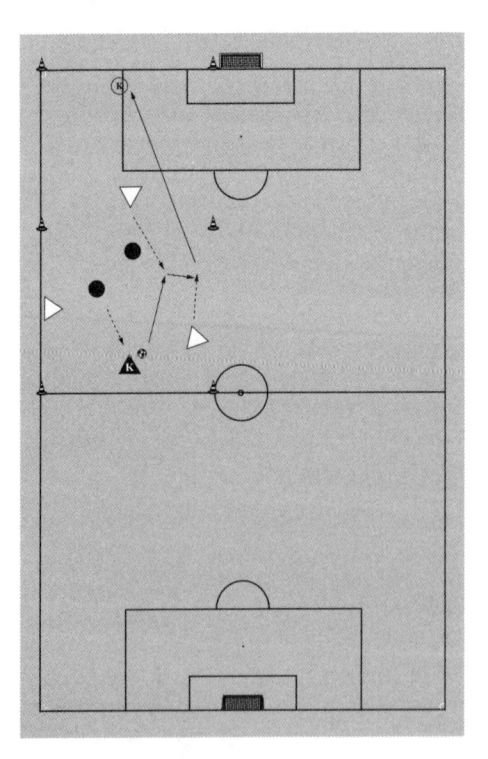

Organization:
- The team of 5 (of which 2 are goalkeepers) tries to keep possession.
- The team of 2/3 tries to intercept the ball.

Coaching points:
- It is all about getting the ball forward
- Try to play the ball with your first touch, or control it with the first touch and play it with the second touch.
- Make sure the ball is ready to be played (not under your body).

Central player
- Call for the ball from your goalkeeper if he is under pressure.

Wide players
- Play the ball in the right direction as you receive it.

Success moment:
If the defenders intercept the ball 3 times (or 4 times), the players switch round.

Section 5 - Coaching Method

Training phase: Line training with 2 lines (6 + K v 4)

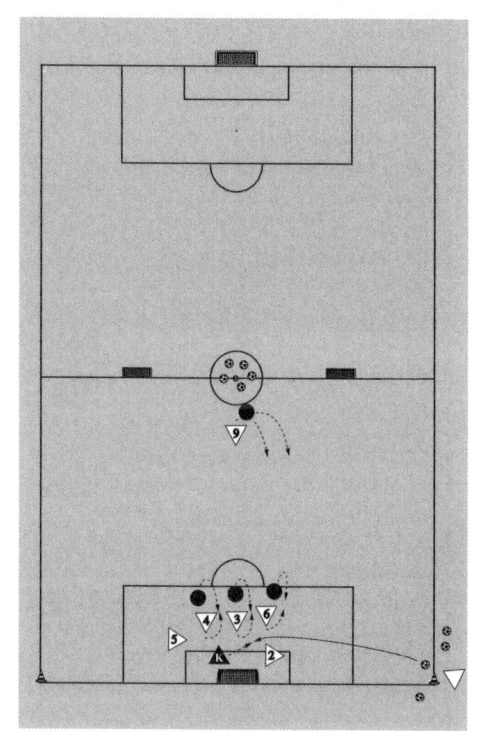

Organization:
We start the training with 2 practical situations:
- A cross
- A backpass

We start again if:
- The ball goes in the corner
- A goal is scored

Coaching points:
After the cross
- We try to play the ball to the most advanced player
- We try to avoid losing possession

After the backpass
Tips for the players:
- Play the ball to the goalkeeper as quickly as possible.
- Play the ball to the goalkeeper so that he can handle it easily (not a bouncing ball).
- Take the goalkeeper's kicking ability into account. Make sure you are immediately available for the goalkeeper to pass the ball back to you.
- Communicate with the goalkeeper.
- Pass the ball at the correct pace – every situation demands its own type of pass.
- Make sure that the goalkeeper can play the ball immediately.

Tips for the goalkeeper:
- Take no risks.
- Decide quickly what you are going to do (before you receive the ball!).
- Decide whether to control the ball with your first touch or play it first-time.
- Communicate with the players as early as possible.
- Only dribble past an opponent in order to get the ball into space.

Game phase:
8v8, depending on the number of available players.
Free play – if the ball goes out for a corner, play restarts with the goalkeeper.

Book 1   Build-Up Play

Session 5

Development objective of the session
Session 5 builds on the previous sessions. The organization of the passing and shooting drill is modified slightly (with 4 goals). The line drill is developed further in the training phase.

Discovery phase:	Positional play (5 v 2/3)
Training phase:	Line training with 2 lines (6 + goalkeeper v 4/5)
Game phase:	Match-related drill (8v8, depending on the number of available players)

Content of the session
Discovery phase: Positional play (5 v 2/3)

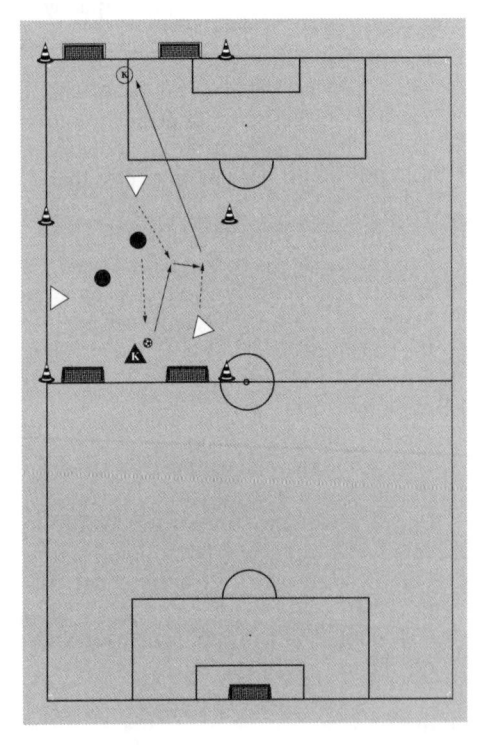

Organization:
- The team of 5 (of which 2 are goalkeepers) tries to keep possession.
- The team of 2/3 tries to intercept the ball.

Coaching points:
- It is all about getting the ball forward
- Try to play the ball with your first touch, or control it with the first touch and play it with the second touch.
- Make sure the ball is ready to be played (not under your body).

Central player
- Call for the ball from your goalkeeper if he is under pressure.

Wide players
- Play the ball in the correct direction as you receive it.

Success moment:
If the defenders score twice, the players switch around.

Section 5 - Coaching Method

Training phase: Line training with 2 lines (6 + K v 4/5)

Organization:
We start the training with 2 practical situations:
- A cross
- A backpass

We start again if:
- The ball goes in the corner
- A goal is scored

Coaching points:
After the cross
- We try to play the ball to the most advanced player
- We try to avoid losing possession

After the backpass
Tips for the players:
- Play the ball to the goalkeeper as quickly as possible.
- Play the ball to the goalkeeper so that he can handle it easily (not a bouncing ball).
- Take the goalkeeper's kicking ability into account. Make sure you are immediately available for the goalkeeper to pass the ball back to you.
- Communicate with the goalkeeper.
- Pass the ball at the correct pace – every situation demands its own type of pass.
- Make sure that the goalkeeper can play the ball immediately.

Tips for the goalkeeper:
- Take no risks.
- Decide quickly what you are going to do (before you receive the ball!).
- Decide whether to control the ball with your first touch or play it first-time.
- Communicate with the players as early as possible.
- Only dribble past an opponent in order to get the ball into space.

Game phase:
8v8, depending on the number of available players.
Free play – if the ball goes out for a corner, play restarts with the goalkeeper.

Book 1   Build-Up Play

Session 6

Development objective of the session
In session 6, the level of difficulty of the drills is increased. The session finishes with a traditional match-related drill.

Discovery phase: Positional play (5 v 3/4)
Training phase: Line training with 2 lines (6 + goalkeeper v 5/6)
Game phase: Match-related drill (8v8, depending on the number of available players)

Content of the session
Discovery phase: Positional play (5 v 3/4)

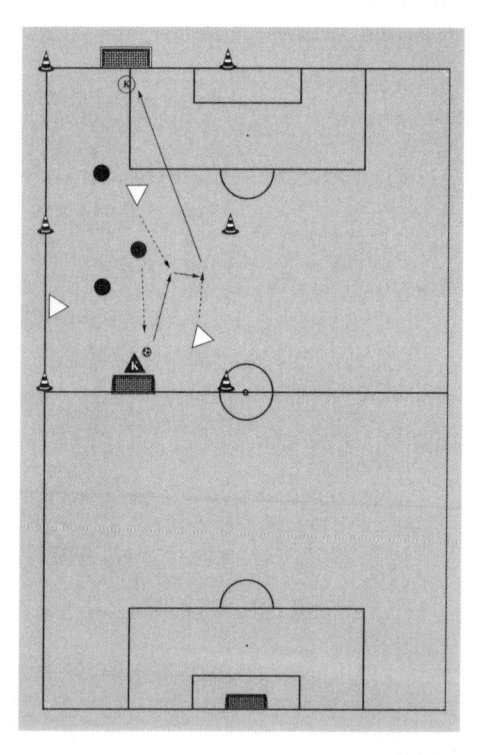

Organization:
- The team of 5 (of which 2 are goalkeepers) tries to keep possession.
- The team of 3/4 tries to intercept the ball.

Coaching points:
- It is all about getting the ball forward
- Try to play the ball with your first touch, or control it with the first touch and play it with the second touch.
- Make sure the ball is ready to be played (not under your body).

Central player
- Call for the ball from your goalkeeper if he is under pressure.

Wide players
- Play the ball in the correct direction as you receive it.

Success moment:
If the defenders score twice, the players switch around.

Section 5 - Coaching Method

Training phase: Line training with 2 lines (6 + K v 5/6)

Organization:
We start the training with 2 practical situations:
- A cross
- A backpass

We start again if:
- The ball goes in the corner
- A goal is scored

Coaching points:
After the cross
- We try to play the ball to the most advanced player
- We try to avoid losing possession

After the backpass
Tips for the players:
- Play the ball to the goalkeeper as quickly as possible.
- Play the ball to the goalkeeper so that he can handle it easily (not a bouncing ball).
- Take the goalkeeper's kicking ability into account. Make sure you are immediately available for the goalkeeper to pass the ball back to you.
- Communicate with the goalkeeper.
- Pass the ball at the correct pace – every situation demands its own type of pass.
- Make sure that the goalkeeper can play the ball immediately.

Tips for the goalkeeper:
- Take no risks.
- Decide quickly what you are going to do (before you receive the ball!).
- Decide whether to control the ball with your first touch or play it first-time.
- Communicate with the players as early as possible.
- Only dribble past an opponent in order to get the ball into space.

Game phase:
8v8, depending on the number of available players.
Free play

Book 1   Build-Up Play

Evaluation

Coaching the aims of the game

Do the players enjoy themselves?
Is there sufficient variation in the drills (match-related drills, finishing)?

Is the development objective achieved?
The players' performance in real matches demonstrates that they have been influenced. The goalkeeper and defenders succeed in building up moves from the back. The players have clearly gone through a development process. Clear progress has been made in the different elements of the development objective:
- The build-up from the goalkeeper to the defenders
- The build-up from the defenders to the midfielders
- The backpass

Is the number of practice drills in the training sessions limited?
There should be a maximum of 3 drills in each training session.

Is the number of practice drills in the module limited?
A total of 5 practice drills are integrated in the module. All other drills are derived from these primary drills.

Is there a good balance between match-related and non-match-related drills?
The match-related drills dominate. The non-match-related drills such as passing and shooting drills with finishing are more supportive in nature.

Is there a progressive buildup over a certain period?
Six training sessions are completed over a period of 5 weeks. The level of difficulty of the drills is gradually increased.

Are there sufficient repetitions for the players?
All players are sufficiently involved in each drill.

Is sufficient consideration given to the age group of the players?
The drills used in these practical examples are oriented to the players' age group. The content is adjusted to the age of the players.

Are the drills adjusted to their level?
The drills are applicable at the regional level. If they are too difficult, the coach can easily adjust them.

Do the players have sufficient freedom of movement?
Sufficient free moments are incorporated.

Section 5 - Coaching Method

14-18 YEAR OLDS:
PROBLEM-ORIENTED COACHING

Book 1   Build-Up Play

The 14 to 18-year-old age group

The players
The build-up acquires more adult characteristics. The players have more variation options. A line can be missed out or the play can be switched to the opposite flank more easily. The players have more stamina and are stronger in the tackle, so the resistance factors are different. Opponents sometimes deliberately attempt to disrupt short-passing build-up moves, so other solutions have to be found. The players must be able to adjust their own capabilities in the build-up play to the strengths and weaknesses of their own team, their opponents and the match situation.

14 to 16-year-olds: Players in this age group are sometimes over enthusiastic in training sessions and matches. Awareness of the game situation and patience in the build-up play can play a crucial role in this age group.

17 and 18-year-olds: The play is more thoughtful and the build-up has a more adult character.

Training sessions
The first phase can include small drills (positional training) and passing and shooting drills. However, drills with 2 lines are preferable. Drills with 3 lines are ideal for perfecting 11v11 at this age. At the end of the session, games of 8v8 or 11v11 can incorporate tasks or success moments to stimulate aspects of build-up play. This age group can be confronted with real match situations (opponents playing in different formations) and different ways of playing (opponents who put pressure on them, opponents who hold off, waiting to exploit a mistake).

14 to 16-year-olds: The coach takes a stricter approach to the build-up play. The players must take as few risks as possible during the build-up play, while taking account of the individual characteristics of each player.

Confront the players with opponents playing in different formations.

At this age, the choices that the players make during the build-up play must increasingly contribute to the match result.

17 and 18-year-olds: These players must be able to give everything in a training session. The level of intensity approaches that of a real match. The build-up training is totally aligned to winning. The coach allows no exceptions to the build-up philosophy.

The coach
Even in this phase where winning is more important, the coach must hold to his coaching philosophy.

14 to 16-year-olds: The players have more insight, so the coach can confront them with the various options that arise during the build-up. He can "correct" the players and then give them their head.

17 and 18-year-olds: In the final phase of their soccer education, the coach can treat the players as if they are adults. The players are given specific tasks, The coach's approach is aligned to winning. The pressure on the players is equivalent to that on players at the adult level.

The match
14 to 16-year-olds: Matches between players in this age group are often highly charged. The players' runs with the ball during the build-up play are not always productive. The players must learn how to cope with the various phases of the match, and learn how to turn them to their own advantage. If the opposing team plays a pressing game, for example, it will not be able to keep up the high level of physical exertion forever. Eventually it will become easier to build up moves by means of short passes. Aspects such as this are typical at this age.

17 and 18-year-olds: The over-enthusiastic approach of the 14 to 16-year-olds is a thing of the past. The players can ration their energy more sensibly and are more capable of taking correct decisions. At this age it is sometimes easier to build up the play via the defenders.

Section 5 - Coaching Method

Aim

> *The build-up module between 14 and 18*
>
> *Aim:*
> - *To perfect playing 11v11*
> - *To learn how to deal with the manner in which the opposition plays*
> - *Collective development with regard to*
>   - *the strengths and weaknesses of the players' own team and the opposition*
>   - *the players' own positions, the line, the total team*

Drills for the discovery phase

Passing and shooting drills	Positional training	Line training 2 lines	Line training 3 lines
	2 : 1 =>	6 : 4 =>	8 : 6 =>
	2 : 2 =>	6 : 5 =>	8 : 7 =>
	3 : 2 =>	6 : 6 =>	8 : 8 =>
	3 : 2 =>	7 : 5 =>	9 : 6 =>
	3 : 3 =>	7 : 6 =>	9 : 7 =>
	4 : 2 =>	7 : 7 =>	9 : 8 =>
	4 : 3 =>	8 : 7 =>	9 : 9 =>
	4 : 4 =>		10 : 8 =>
	5 : 4 =>		10 : 9 =>
			10 : 10 =>
			11 : 10 =>

Training phase

Line training 2 lines	Line training 3 lines
6 : 4 =>	8 : 6 =>
6 : 5 =>	8 : 7 =>
6 : 6 =>	8 : 8 =>
7 : 5 =>	9 : 6 =>
7 : 6 =>	9 : 7 =>
7 : 7 =>	9 : 8 =>
8 : 7 =>	9 : 9 =>
	10 : 8 =>
	10 : 9 =>
	10 : 10 =>
	11 : 10 =>

Game phase

> *Match-related drills (8v8 to 11 v11, depending on number of available players)*

Book 1   Build-Up Play

Practical example
Problem-oriented coaching
As the players get older, we talk of "problem-oriented coaching". The players have played 11v11 for a number of years and have built up a basic knowledge of the manner of playing. The coach can therefore base his coaching more on real match situations. The players know the aims of the build-up play and the coach can treat them in more detail.

Problem-oriented coaching

Problem-oriented coaching involves the following steps.
First we determine:
- The age group
- The level
- The number of training sessions per week
- The starting level of the players
- The soccer problem – who, what, where, when?
- The development objective – what do we want to achieve?

We then choose the following steps:
1. What playing system are we going to choose?
2. Which module do we want to choose?
3. Which players are we looking at?
4. Which part of the field and in which direction?
5. What drills should we choose?
6. How should we factor in the age-typical aspects?
7. How should we draw up the schedule?
8. What should be the content of the training session?

We determine
The starting situation:

Age group: 16 year olds
Level: Regional amateur level
Number of training sessions per week: 2
Starting level of the players: The players know the aims of the build-up play.

Soccer problem
The opposing team is defensively inclined. It plays in a well organized block around the center circle and waits for a chance to counter-attack. Our own players are tempted too often to pass the ball forward, so we lose possession too often. In particular, passes to the attackers regularly go astray.

The development objective
The build-up from the defenders to the attackers

1. What playing system are we going to choose?
The players are familiar with a 1-3-4-3 formation.

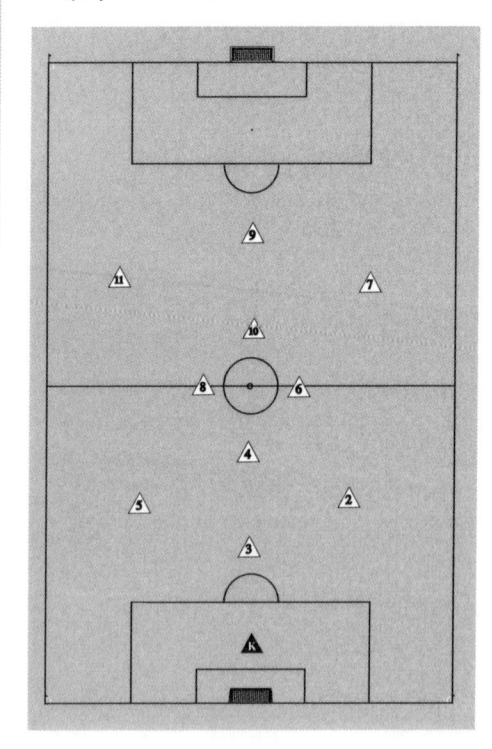

Section 5 - Coaching Method

2. Which module do we want to choose?
The build-up module.

3. Which players are we looking at?
Mainly the goalkeeper and the defenders in relation to the midfielders and attackers.

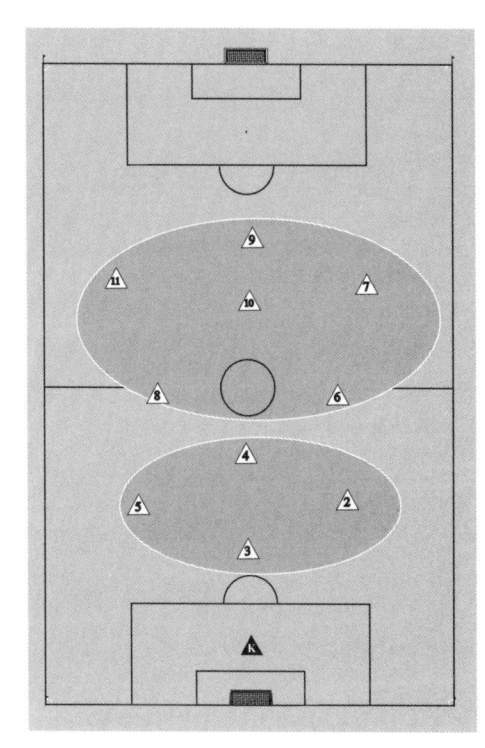

4. Which part of the field and in which direction?
In the players' own half and part of the opposition's half. We play from a fixed goal in the direction of the midfield.

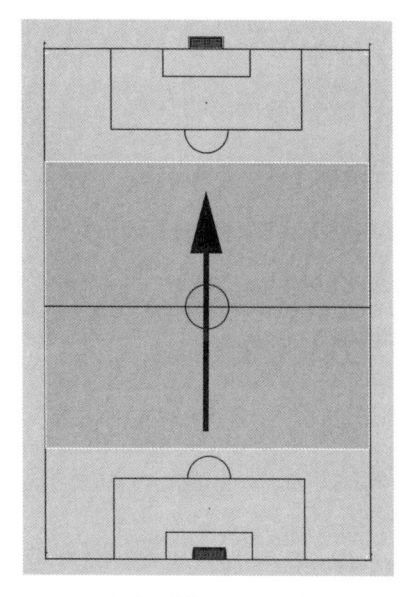

5. What drills should we choose?
The following drills can be used for the 14 to 18-year-old age group:
- Passing and shooting drills.
- Positional training (from 2v1 to 5v5).
- Line training with 2 lines (from 5v5 to 8v8).
- Line training with 3 lines (from 8v7 to 11v11).

Problem-oriented coaching mainly makes use of match-related drills.

6. How should we factor in the age-typical aspects?
In the oldest age group, the emphasis is on specialization in the player's own position. The positions that a player occupies during training sessions corresponds as far as possible to his strongest position.

7. How should we draw up the schedule?
This schedule can be used as a basis by the coach.

Book 1   Build- Up Play

Saturday – The match
In the match, the coach is confronted with the following soccer problem:
The opposing team is defensively inclined. It plays in a well organized block around the center circle and waits for a chance to counter-attack. Our own players are tempted too often to pass the ball forward, so we lose possession too often. In particular, passes to the attackers regularly go astray.

Tuesday	**training**	**tactical**	**build-up**	**session 1**
Thursday	**training**	**tactical**	**build-up**	**session 2**
Saturday	In the match, the build-up play is more patient. In the second half, however, the players revert to their old habits; under pressure, they are too quick to play the ball forward.			
Tuesday	**training**	**tactical**	**build-up**	**session 3**
Thursday	training	Positional play and match-related drill		
Saturday	match			
Tuesday	training	Finishing drill and match-related drill		
Thursday	**training**	**tactical**	**build-up**	**session 4**
Saturday	match	The build-up from the back is again at an acceptable level		

Section 5 - Coaching Method

8. What should be the content of the training session?
We have put together 4 imaginary training sessions.

The development objectives of the training sessions.
In **session 1** we start with a passing and shooting drill, with the focus on acting quickly before playing the ball forward. In the training phase we have a positional game of 6v3 with 3 teams, in which the players learn how to remain patient in possession. We end the session with a match-related drill.

In **session 2** we go further with the passing and shooting drill. We then choose another drill with 2 lines. We try to translate into practice the technical aspects of the passing and shooting drill and the tactical tips from the positional game in the previous session. The emphasis is on remaining patient and not kicking the ball forward too hastily. We end the session with a match-related drill. One team plays defensively and the other tries to build up the play efficiently.

Session 3: In the match, the build-up play is more patient. In the second half, however, the players revert to their old habits; under pressure, they are too quick to play the ball forward. We start the session with a positional game of 6v3 with 3 teams. To increase the pressure we have made the playing area smaller. In the training phase we switch to a drill with 2 lines. Here, too, the level of difficulty is increased. The players can score in 3 goals rather than 4. We end with a free match-related drill.

Session 4: In the first phase we create a positional game with higher levels of difficulty. Here, too, the focus is on waiting for the right moment. In the second phase we switch to a drill with 2 lines. Now the players can score in 2 goals instead of 3. We end with a match-related drill of 11v11. One team takes up positions in its own half and the other team tries to build up the play effectively.

In the match we see that the build-up play proceeds smoothly again.

Book 1   Build-Up Play

Session 1
Development objective of the session
In session 1 we start with a passing and shooting drill, with the focus on acting quickly before playing the ball forward. In the training phase we have a positional game of 6v3 with 3 teams, in which the players learn how to remain patient in possession. We end the session with a match-related drill.

Discovery phase: Passing and shooting drill
Training phase: Positional game (6v3 with 3 teams)
Game phase: Match-related drill (8v8, depending on the number of available players)

Content of the session
Discovery phase:
Passing and shooting drill

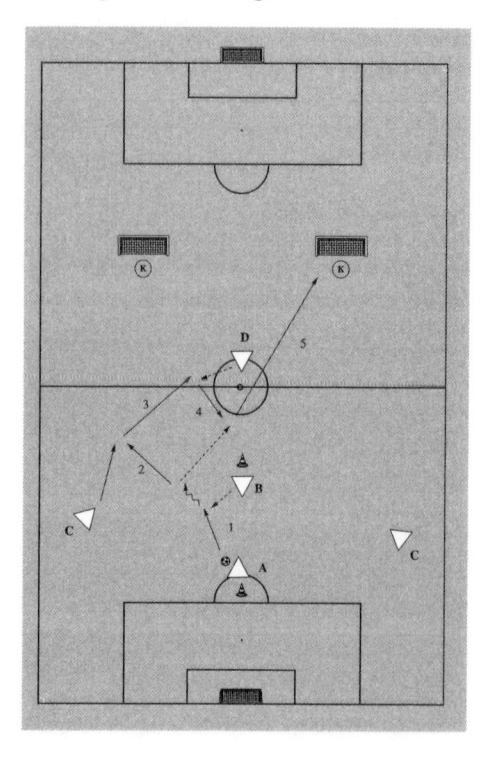

Organization:
- The central defender plays the ball to the defensive midfielder (1).
- The defensive midfielder turns and passes to the left back (2).
- The left back plays a first-time pass to the striker (3).
- The striker lays the ball off to the defensive midfielder (4), who has made a forward run in support.
- The midfielder shoots at the goal on the right.

We then start on the other flank.
The players either change positions (A goes to B, B to C, C to D and D to A) or stay in their fixed positions.

Coaching points:
The aim of this drill is to increase the efficiency of passing and shooting and, especially, the speed of execution.

Player A
- Play the ball to the defensive midfielder so that he can control it as easily as possible.
- Play the ball firmly.
- Communicate with the player in front of you.

Player B
- Turn quickly.
- Pass the ball into the space in front of the left back so that he has the time to play the ball forward with his first touch.
- Do not hit the pass too hard.
- Run onto the ball.
- Shoot with your first touch.

Player C
- Leave space in front of you.
- Observe the situation in front of you (where is the striker?).
- Play the ball firmly to the striker.

Player D
- Lay the ball off accurately.
- Ensure that the ball can be played immediately.
- Ensure that your marker cannot intercept the lay-off.

Section 5 - Coaching Method

Training phase: 6v3 with 3 teams

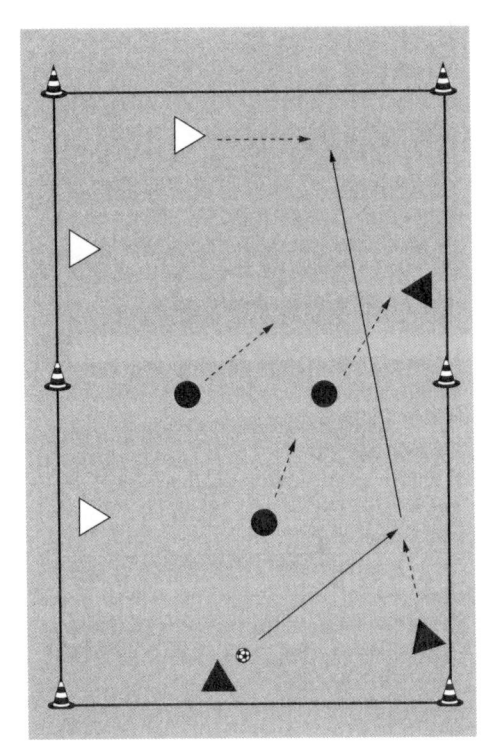

Organization:
We play 6v3 with 3 teams. The team that sends the ball out of play or loses possession goes into the middle. The switch is made immediately.
- Free play
- Two-touch play

Coaching points:
- Remain patient on the ball.
- Defenders nearby = Try to pass the ball forward.
- Defenders further away = Circulate the ball.

Success moment:
Every 30 seconds, the coach notes which team is in the middle. When one of the teams has defended 5 times, it is the loser.

Game phase:
8v8 (depending on the number of available players).
Free play.

Book 1   Build-Up Play

Session 2
Development objective of the session
In session 2 we go further with the passing and shooting drill. We then choose another drill with 2 lines. We try to translate into practice the technical aspects of the passing and shooting drill and the tactical tips from the positional game in the previous session. The emphasis is on remaining patient and not kicking the ball forward too hastily. We end the session with a match-related drill. One team plays defensively and the other tries to build up the play efficiently.

Discovery phase: Passing and shooting drill
Training phase: Line training with 2 lines (8+GK v 6)
Game phase: Match-related drill (11v11, depending on the number of available players)

Content of the session
Discovery phase:
Passing and shooting drill

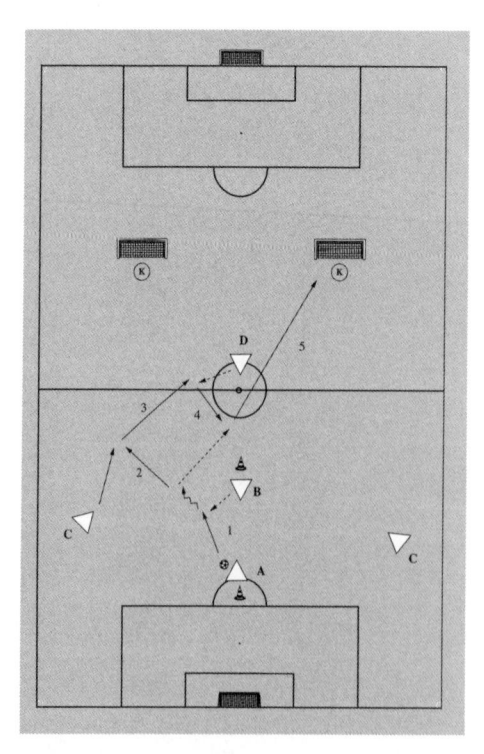

Organization:
- The central defender plays the ball to the defensive midfielder (1).
- The defensive midfielder turns and passes to the left back (2).
- The left back plays a first-time pass to the striker (3).
- The striker lays the ball off to the defensive midfielder (4), who has made a forward run in support.
- The midfielder shoots at the goal on the right.

We then start on the other flank.
The players either change positions (A goes to B, B to C, C to D and D to A) or stay in their fixed positions.

Coaching points:
The aim of this drill is to increase the efficiency of passing and shooting and, especially, the speed of execution.

Player A
- Play the ball to the defensive midfielder so that he can control it as easily as possible.
- Play the ball firmly.
- Communicate with the player in front of you.

Player B
- Turn quickly.
- Pass the ball into the space in front of the left back so that he has the time to play the ball forward with his first touch.
- Do not hit the pass too hard.
- Run onto the ball.
- Shoot with your first touch.

Player C
- Leave space in front of you.
- Observe the situation in front of you (where is the striker?).
- Play the ball firmly to the striker.

Player D
- Lay the ball off accurately.
- Ensure that the ball can be played immediately.
- Ensure that your marker cannot intercept the lay-off.

Section 5 - Coaching Method

Training phase:
Line training with 2 lines (8 + GK v 6)

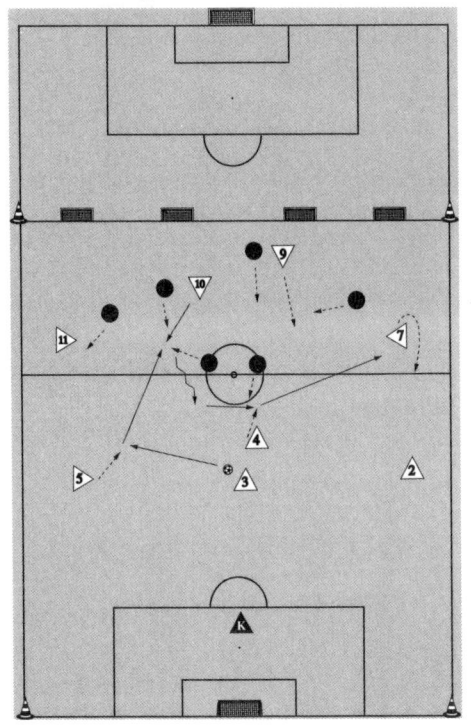

Organization:
The team of 8 tries to score in one of the 4 goals. The team of 6 plays defensively in a disciplined block. They wait for a mistake so that they can counterattack.

Coaching points:
The 8 attackers
- Keep the field as wide as possible.
- Be patient – no unnecessary loss of possession.
- Tempt the opposition out of its defensive block.
- Circulate the ball – wait for the right moment to pass it forward.
- Always be aware of the danger of losing the ball.

Game phase:
11v11 (against a younger or older team)
- The opposing team positions itself around the center circle and waits for an opportunity to counterattack.
- The team in possession tries to build up patiently.

105

Book 1   Build-Up Play

Session 3
Development objective of the session
Session 3: In the match, the build-up play is more patient. In the second half, however, the players revert to their old habits; under pressure, they are too quick to play the ball forward. We start the session with a positional game of 6v3 with 3 teams. To increase the pressure we have made the playing area smaller. In the training phase we switch to a drill with 2 lines. Here, too, the level of difficulty is increased. The players can score in 3 goals rather than 4. We end with a free match-related drill.

Discovery phase:	6v3 with 3 teams
Training phase:	Line training with 2 lines (8+GK v 6)
Game phase:	Match-related drill (8v8, depending on the number of available players)

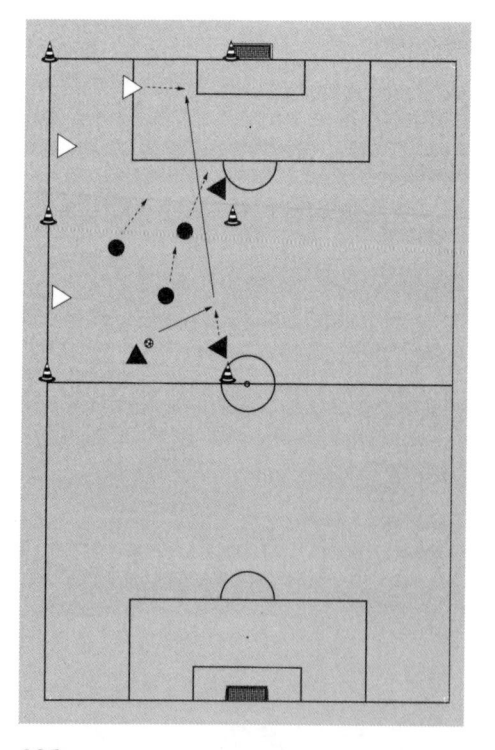

Organization:
We play 6v3 with 3 teams. The team that sends the ball out of play or loses possession goes into the middle. The switch is made immediately.
- Free play
- Two-touch play

Coaching points:
- Remain patient on the ball.
- Defenders nearby = Try to pass the ball forward.
- Defenders further away = Circulate the ball.

Success moment
Every 30 seconds, the coach notes which team is in the middle. When one of the teams has defended 5 times, it is the loser.

Content of the session
Discovery phase:
6v3 with 3 teams

Section 5 - Coaching Method

Training phase:
Line training with 2 lines (8 + GK v 6)

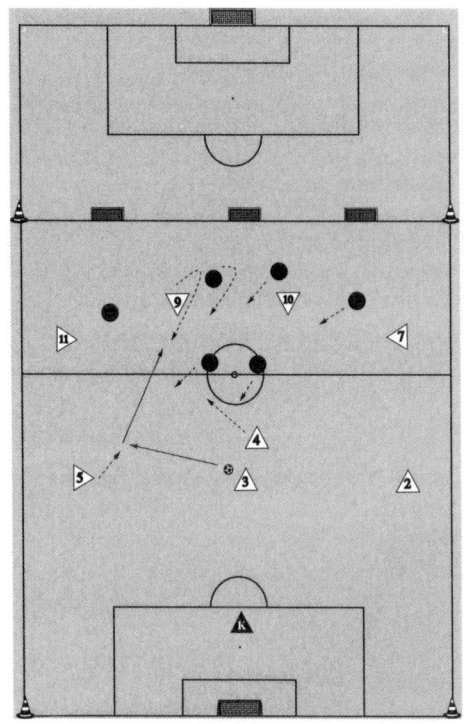

Organization:
The team of 8 tries to score in one of the 4 goals. The team of 6 plays defensively in a disciplined block. They wait for a mistake so that they can counterattack.

Coaching points:
The 8 attackers
- Keep the field as wide as possible.
- Be patient – no unnecessary loss of possession.
- Tempt the opposition out of its defensive block.
- Circulate the ball – wait for the right moment to pass it forward.
- Always be aware of the danger of losing the ball.

Game phase:
8v8 (depending on the number of available players).
Free play – if the ball goes out for a corner, play restarts with the goalkeeper.

Book 1 Build-Up Play

Session 4
Development objective of the session
Session 4: In the first phase we create a positional game with higher levels of difficulty. Here, too, the focus is on waiting for the right moment. In the second phase we switch to a drill with 2 lines. Now the players can score in 2 goals instead of 3. We end with a match-related drill of 11v11. One team takes up positions in its own half and the other team tries to build up the play effectively.

Discovery phase:	5v4 with 2 zones
Training phase:	Line training with 2 lines (8+GK v 6)
Game phase:	Match-related drill (11v11, against a younger or older team)

Content of the session
Discovery phase:
5v4 with 2 zones

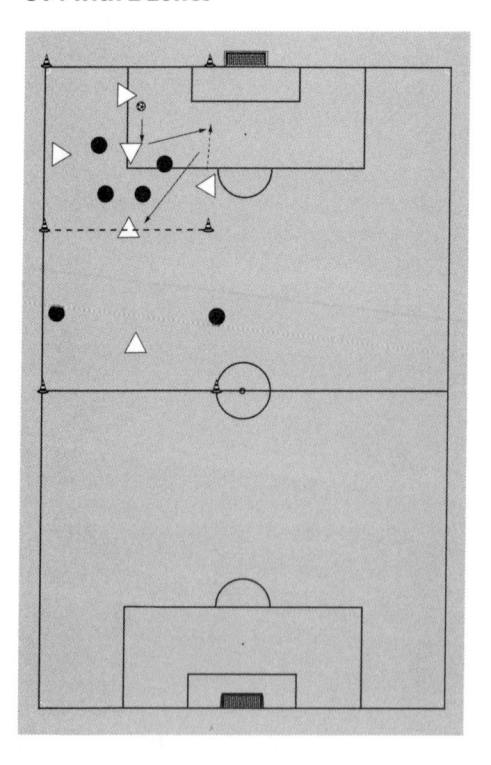

Organization:
The team of 5 tries to keep possession. The players in the team of 4 try to intercept the ball and play it past the defender to their teammates in the other zone.

We then create the same situation in the other zone.
- Ensure that the zone is big enough.

Coaching points:
- Try to be aware of the game situation.
- Be aware of the position of the defender.
- Defenders nearby = Try to pass the ball forward.
- Defenders further away = Circulate the ball.

Section 5 - Coaching Method

Training phase:
Line training with 2 lines (8 + GK v 6)

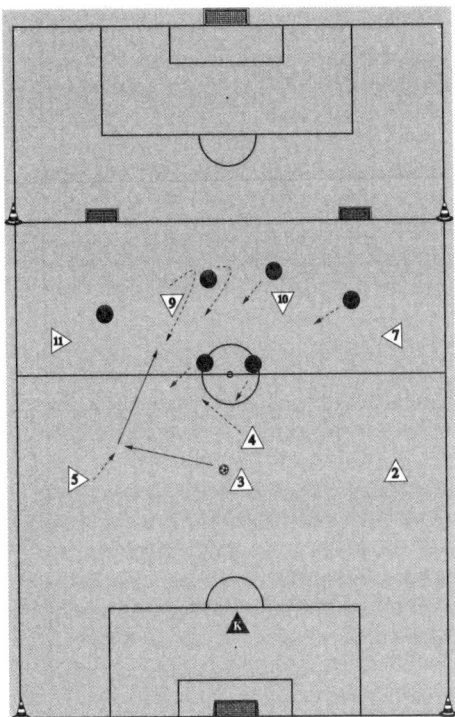

Organization:
The team of 8 tries to score in one of the 4 goals. The team of 6 plays defensively in a disciplined block. They wait for a mistake so that they can counterattack.

Coaching points:
The 8 attackers
- Keep the field as wide as possible.
- Be patient – no unnecessary loss of possession.
- Tempt the opposition out of its defensive block.
- Circulate the ball – wait for the right moment to pass it forward.
- Always be aware of the danger of losing the ball.

Game phase:
11v11 (against a younger or older team).

Task
The opposing team plays defensively and waits for an opportunity to take advantage of a mistake.

Book 1   Build-Up Play

Evaluation

Problem-oriented coaching

Has there been an influence on the soccer problem?
Clear progress can be observed in matches. The players have clearly been influenced, as can be seen from the build-up play from the defenders to the attackers.

Is the number of practice drills in the training sessions limited?
There are a maximum of 3 drills in each training session.

Is the number of practice drills in the module limited?
A total of 5 practice drills are integrated in the module. All other drills are derived from these primary drills.

Is there a good balance between match-related and non-match-related drills?
Because of the nature of the soccer problem, only match-related drills are used.

Is there a progressive buildup over a certain period?
Four training sessions are completed over a period of 2 weeks. The level of difficulty of the drills is gradually increased.

Are there sufficient repetitions for the players?
All players are sufficiently involved in each drill.

Is sufficient consideration given to the age group of the players?
The drills used in these practical examples are oriented to the players' age group. The content is adjusted to the age of the players.

Are the drills adjusted to their level?
The drills are applicable at the regional level. If they are too difficult, the coach can easily adjust them.

Do the players have sufficient freedom of movement?
Sufficient free moments are incorporated.

Section 6 - Practice Drills

Practice Drills

Book 1 Build-Up Play

Passing and Shooting Drills

Passing and shooting drill

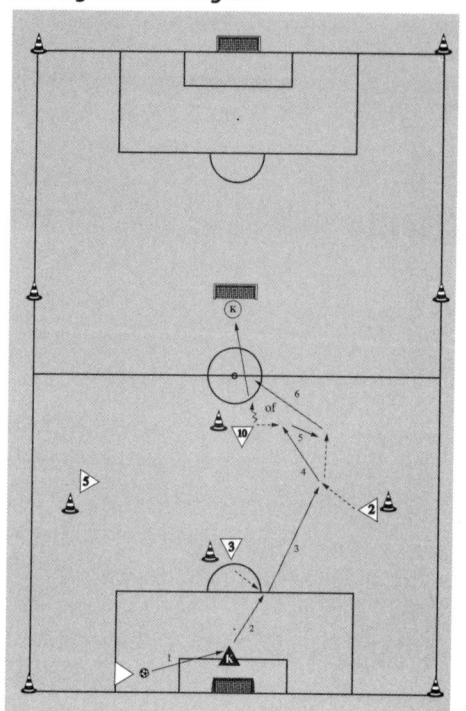

Development objective
Build up from the goalkeeper to the central defender, and the continuation.

Organization
- Player A passes to the goalkeeper.
- The goalkeeper positions the ball in front of his kicking foot and passes to the central defender (3).
- The central defender (3) turns and passes to the right or left back (2 or 5).
- The right or left back (2 or 5) passes to the withdrawn striker (10).
- The withdrawn striker lays the ball off or shoots at goal.

Build up over both flanks.
The players all move up one position, following the ball.

Success moment
10 balls. How often is a goal scored?

Coaching points
A - Firm cross
The goalkeeper
- Position the ball in front of your kicking foot.
- Pass the ball so that central defender can control it as easily as possible.

The central defender (3)
- Make a diagonal run way from the player you are marking.
- Stand at an angle to the path of the ball.
- Use your outside foot to control the ball.

The right and left backs (2 and 5)
- Stand at an angle to the path of the ball.
- Check away from the ball and back again.
- Try to play as far forward as possible.

The withdrawn striker (10)
- Check away from the ball and back again.
- Control the ball with your first touch.

Section 6 - Practice Drills

Passing and shooting drill

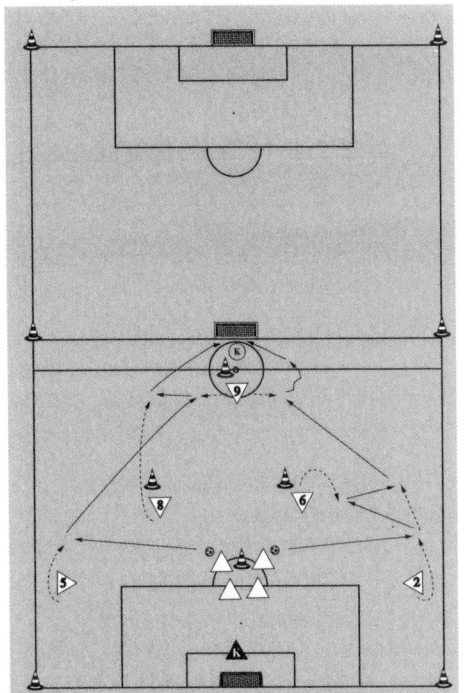

Development objective
Build up via the right and left backs.

Organization
A) (see diagram)
- The central defender (3) passes to the right back (2).
- The right back (2) passes to the right midfielder (6).
- The right midfielder passes back to the right back.
- The right back (2) passes to the striker (9).
- The striker (9) turns and shoots.

B) (see diagram) Similar to A, except that the build-up is down the left flank, the left back (5) misses out the midfielder, and the striker (9) lays the ball off to the left midfielder (8), who has made a forward run in support.

C)
- The ball is played to the right midfielder (6), who turns with the ball.
- He passes to the striker (9).
- The striker (9) turns with the ball or lays it off to the right midfielder (6).

D) The players make their own choice (they communicate with each other).

Coaching points
The central defender (3)
- Play the ball into the space in front of 2 & 5.

The right and left backs (2 and 5)
- Stand at an angle to the path of the ball.
- Look upfield.
- Firm pass.
- Communicate with the midfielder/striker.

The right and left midfielders (6 and 8)
- Make a diagonal run away from your marker.
- Stand at an angle to the path of the ball.

The striker (9)
- Do not move too fast toward the ball.
- Ensure that the lay-off is easy to handle.

Book 1   Build-Up Play

Passing and shooting drill

Development objective
Passing to the central defender and building up the play down the center.

Organization
- The goalkeeper passes to the central defender.
- The central defender (3) turns with the ball and passes to the withdrawn striker (10), who has dropped back.
- The withdrawn striker (10) lays the ball off to the defensive midfielder (4).
- The defensive midfielder (4) scores in the small goal.

The central defender makes himself available on the right and on the left alternately. (Build-up on the right and left alternately.)

Success moment
The players must shoot first-time at the small goals. 20 balls = 15 goals.

Coaching points
The goalkeeper
- Play the ball to the central defender so that he can control it as easily as possible.
- Communicate with the defender.

The central defender (3)
- Turn with the ball.
- Control the ball with the outside foot.
- Look for space.

The defensive midfielder (4)
- Choose the right moment to make a forward run.
- Look for space.

The withdrawn striker (10)
- Lay the ball off with the outside foot.
- Make sure that a goal can be scored.

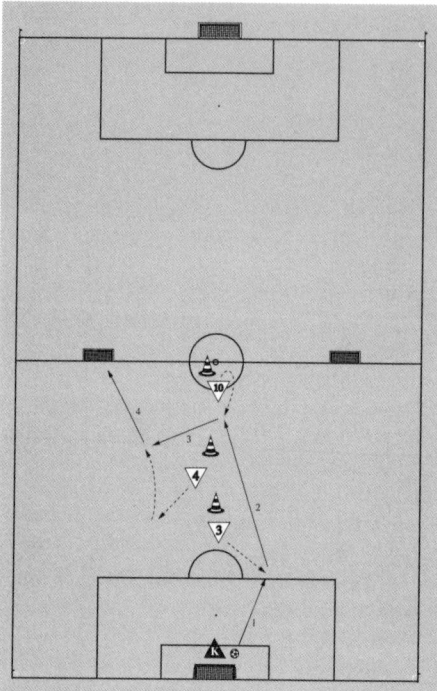

You can work with fixed groups of 3, who can move up one position after each sequence.

Section 6 - Practice Drills

Passing and shooting drill

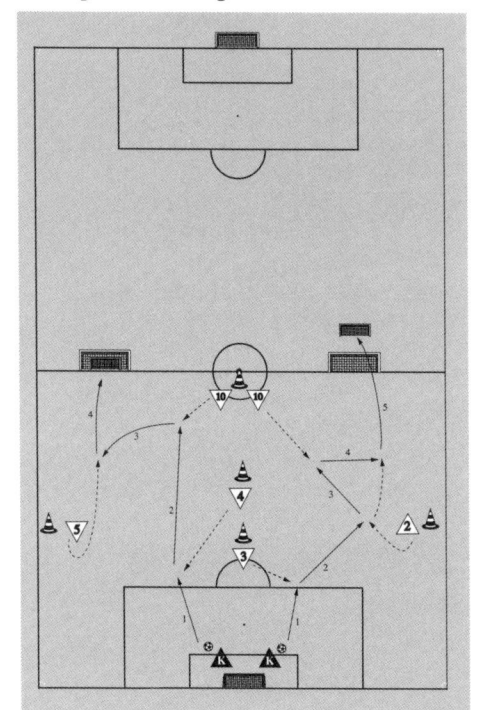

Development objective
Build-up via the central defender.

Organization
We start at the same time on the right and on the left.
Each goalkeeper plays the ball to a central defender (3 or 4).

Option A
- The goalkeeper plays the ball to the central defender (3).
- The central defender (3) passes to the right back (2).
- The right back (2) plays a 1-2 with the withdrawn striker (10).
- The right back (2) tries to chip the ball over the large goal into the small goal.

Option B
- The goalkeeper plays the ball to the central defender (4).
- The central defender (3) passes down the center to the withdrawn striker (10).
- The withdrawn striker (10) lays the ball off to the left back (5), who has made a forward run.
- The left back (3) shoots at the small goal.

Option C
- Own choice

Success moment
20 attempts – how often must a goal be scored?

Coaching points
See previous passing and shooting drills.

Book 1   Build-Up Play

Passing and shooting drill

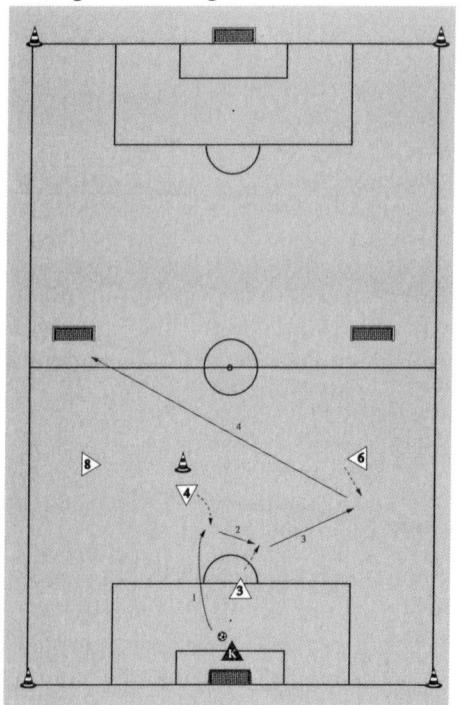

You can place an empty goal in the path of the ball to simulate an opponent.

Development objective
Build-up from the central players to the midfielders and passing to the flank.

Organization
- The goalkeeper plays the ball to the defensive midfielder (4).
- The defensive midfielder (4) lays the ball off the advancing central defender (3).
- The central defender (3) passes to the right midfielder (6).
- The right midfielder (6) controls the ball, turns and shoots diagonally at the large goal.

The defensive midfielder (4) makes himself available on the right and the left alternately (build-up down the right and left alternately).

Coaching points
The goalkeeper
- Distance (roll or throw the ball).
- Communicate with the defensive midfielder.
The defensive midfielder (4)
- Lay the ball off so that the defender can control it easily.
- Lay the ball off with the outside foot.
The central defender (3)
- Don't move too quickly toward the ball.
- Look for space.
- Play the ball firmly.
- Communicate with the midfielder.
The right and left midfielders (6 and 8)
- Look over your shoulder.
- Turn quickly.
- Control the ball with your first touch.
- Shoot with your instep; not too high.

Section 6 - Practice Drills

Passing and shooting drill

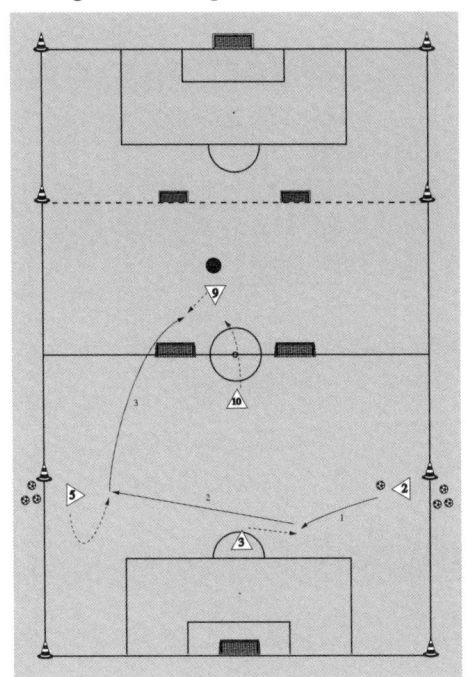

Development objective
Switching the play to the other flank and playing the ball through the air to the advanced striker.

Organization
- The right back (2) plays the ball to the central defender (3).
- The central defender (3) plays the ball through the air to the advanced striker (9).
- When the striker receives the ball, the defender joins in the play and the withdrawn striker (10) moves up in support.
- We then play 2v1.
- The attackers score in one of the smal goals.
- The defender scores by running with the ball between the two large goals.

We start on the right and left alternately.

Success moment
12 long balls. How often do the attackers score?

Coaching points
The right back (2)
- Pass the ball firmly.
- Play the ball into the space in front of the central defender.

The central defender (3)
- Leave the space open.
- Play the ball into the space in front of the left back (5).

The left back (5)
- Look for space.
- Play the ball firmly to the advanced striker.

117

Book 1   Build-Up Play

Positional training

2v1
2v2
3v2
3v3
4v2
4v3
4v4
5v3
5v4
5v5   Game drill

Section 6 - Practice Drills

Positional play – 4v2 with large goal

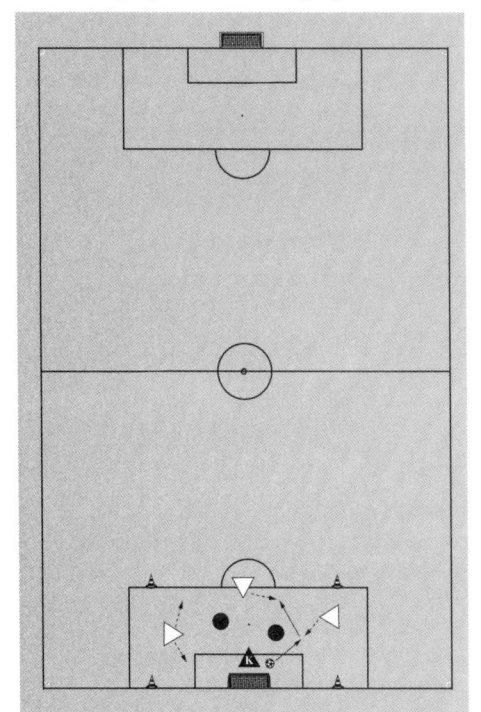

Development objective
Basic principles of positional play

Organization
- The team of 4 tries to keep possession.
- The team of 2 tries to win the ball and score in the large goal.

Success moment
Attackers: Circulate the ball 5 times.
Defenders: Goal = 2 points.

Coaching points
Attackers
- See basics of positional play on page …
- Loss of possession = Defend immediately

Book 1   Build-Up Play

2 + K v 1

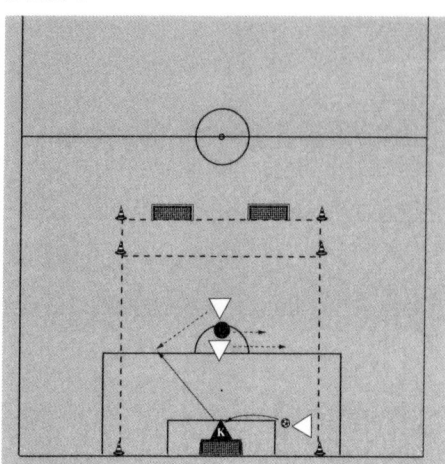

Development objective
Basic principles of build-up play.

Organization
- The drill starts when the ball is played to the goalkeeper.
- The goalkeeper controls the ball.
- We then play 2v1.
- The team of 2 can score by taking the ball over the imaginary line and shooting into one of the 2 goals.
- The opposing player can score in the large goal. After a goal is scored the players change positions.

Success moment
Goals by the opposing player count double.

Coaching points
- The 2 defenders stand on the flank at an angle to the path of the ball and use the outside foot to receive the ball.
- The goalkeeper tries to be always available to receive a backpass.
- The goalkeeper tries to pass as far forward as possible to the defenders.

2 + K v 2

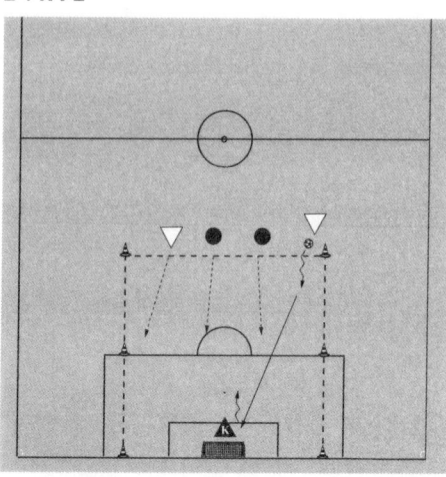

Development objective
Basic principles of build-up play after the ball is played back.

Organization
- The drill starts when the ball is played to the goalkeeper.
- In cooperation with the goalkeeper, the goalkeeper's two teammates try to take up positions in space.
- These 2 players score by taking the ball over the line.
- The 2 opposing players score in the large goal.

Success moment
When the opposing players score, they switch roles with the other 2 players.

Coaching points
- See coaching instructions – The backpass.
- The goalkeeper goes forward with the ball at his feet to create a 3v2 situation and thus create space for one of his defenders.

Section 6 - Practice Drills

3 + K v 2

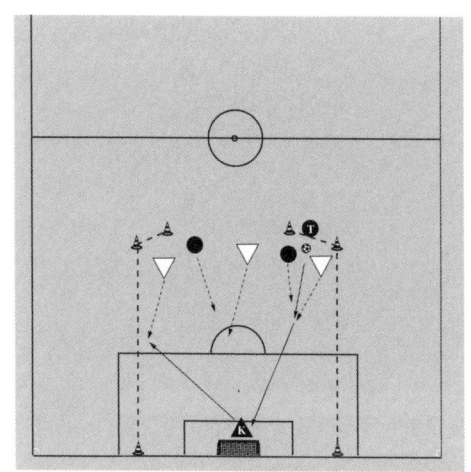

Development objective
Basic principles of the backpass.

Organization
- The drill starts when the coach plays the ball between the 2 players. The player belonging to the team of 3 has a 2-yard start.
- One of the players of the team of 3 passes the ball back to the goalkeeper and we then play 3 v 2 + goalkeeper.
- The 2 players can score in the large goal.
- The 3 players can score by taking the ball between one of the 2 pairs of cones.

Success moment
Who is the first to score 5 goals?

Coaching points
- Basic principles of the backpass.
- The goalkeeper goes forward with the ball at his feet to create a 3v2 situation and thus create space for one of his defenders.
- The 2 defenders stand on the flank at an angle to the path of the ball and use the outside foot to receive the ball.
- The goalkeeper tries to be always available to receive a backpass.
- The central players calls for a diagonal pass and stands at an angle to the path of the ball as he receives it.

3 + K v 3

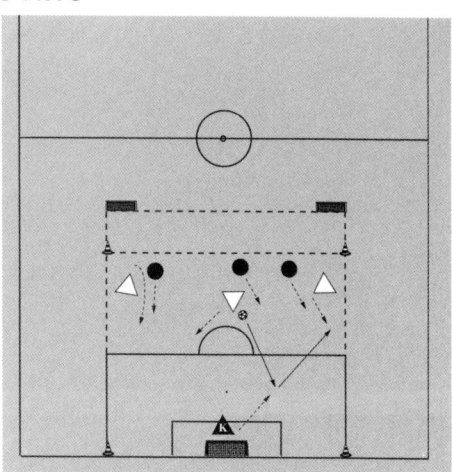

Development objective
Basic principles of build-up play.

Organization
- The teammates of the goalkeeper can score in one of the 2 small goals beyond the imaginary line.
- Their opponents can score in the large goal.
- The goalkeeper can score by kicking the ball out into one of the small goals.

Success moment
A goal scored by the goalkeeper counts double.

Coaching points
- The goalkeeper goes forward with the ball at his feet to create space for one of his defenders.
More options!
The option that gets the ball furthest forward is always to be preferred.
- Pass to the feet of the player on the flank.
- Pass into space ahead of the player on the flank.
- Long ball into a small goal.

Book 1   Build-Up Play

4 + K v 2

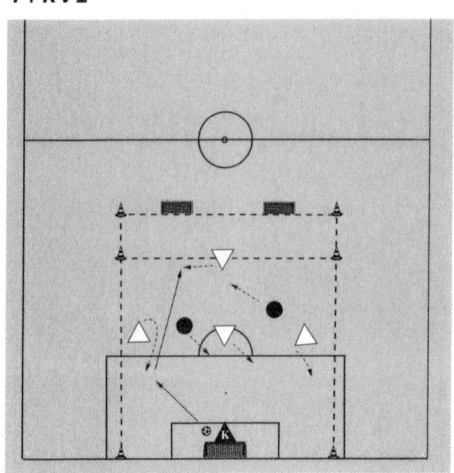

4 + K v 3

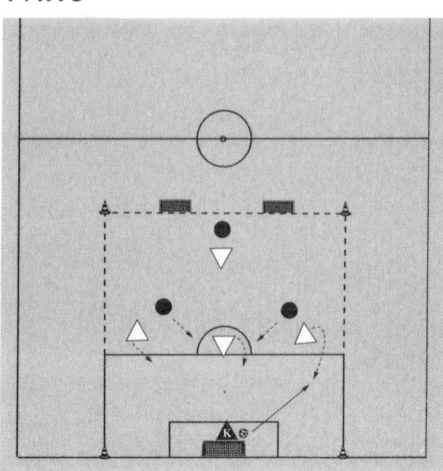

Development objective
Basic principles of build-up play.

Organization
- We play 3 + goalkeeper v 2.
- The team of 3 and the goalkeeper try to play the ball to the striker on the imaginary line.
- A goal can only be scored after the ball has been played to the striker.
- The team of 2 can score in the large goal.

Success moment
A goal scored by the following build-up counts double: long ball from goalkeeper to striker; lay-off to player running forward in support; shot at goal.

Coaching points
- The goalkeeper can also play the ball to the advanced striker.
- The striker and the defender position themselves so that both available to receive a pass when the goalkeeper has the ball.

Development objective
Basic principles of build-up play.

Organization
- The goalkeeper has the ball.
- Each player on the team of 4 has a number. The coach calls a number and the player with this number must then make himself available to receive the ball. The goalkeeper must decide whether he can pass to the player. After the first touch of the ball, the other players join in.
- The team of 4 score in one of the small goals.
- The team of 3 scores in the large goal.

Success moment
A goal scored by a move built up from the back counts double.

Coaching points
- The goalkeeper tries to create space for the defender.
More options!
- Pass to the feet of the player on the flank.
- Pass into space ahead of the player on the flank.
- ...

Section 6 - Practice Drills

4 + K v 4 + K

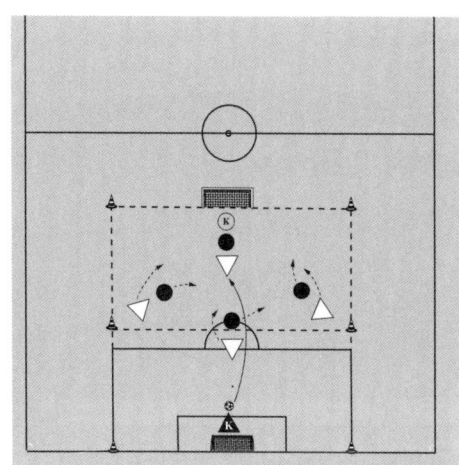

Game drill 5 v 5

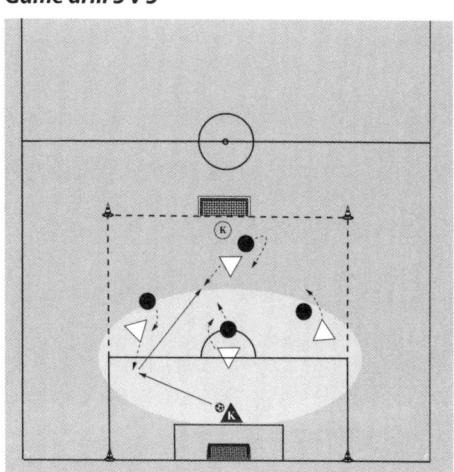

Development objective
Basic principles of build-up play.

Organization
- A team can score when it is in possession in the opposition's half.
- A goalkeeper can score by kicking a long ball into the opposing team's goal (in this case the opposing goalkeeper is not allowed to defend his goal).

Success moment
Who is the first to score 5 goals? A goal scored by a long kick from the goalkeeper counts double. A goal can only be scored when all of the players have crossed the center line.

Coaching points
- If more than one option is available, choose the one that gets the ball furthest forward.
- Make yourself available for a pass.
- Run into space.
- Who is easiest to reach?

Development objective
Encouraging the goalkeeper to take the initiative when he has the ball.

Organization
Task:
- Aim: To encourage the goalkeeper to take the initiative.
  - When the goalkeeper has the ball, he goes forward with the ball at his feet and tries to pass to the advanced striker. The central defender tries to get into space.

If a team wins a corner or a throw in, its goalkeeper restarts the play

Success moment
All goals scored after a build-up move started by the goalkeeper count double.

Coaching points
- Lose your marker!
- Make yourself available for a pass.

Book 1   **Build-Up Play**

Line training with 2 lines

        6v3
        6v4
        6v5
        6v6
        7v5
        7v6
        7v7
        8v7
        8v8   Game drill

Section 6 - Practice Drills

Positional game (6 v 3/4)

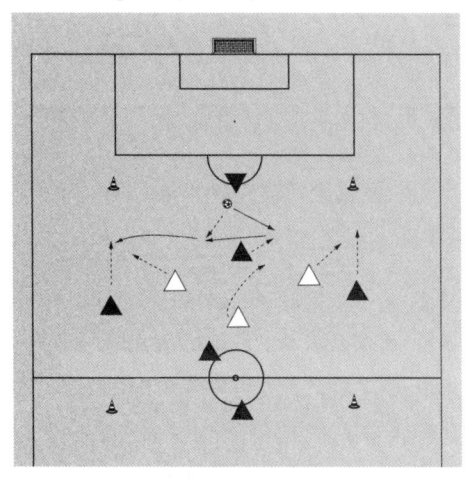

Development objective
Playing a forward pass.

Organization
Field: 30 to 40 yards x 15 to 20 yards.
- The team of 6 tries to keep possession.
- The team of 3 or 4 tries to win possession.
Free play/2-touch play/1-touch play/obligatory 2-touch play/smaller playing area.

Success moment
The coach secretly measures how much time the team of 3 needs to win the ball. The team then has to improve on this time.

Coaching points
- Formation – see diagram.
- The focus is on the forward pass.
- Everything is done with the aim of passing the ball forward (passing back or passing square = preparation for forward pass)
- The forward pass should be played when the defender challenges for the ball.
- Use good positional play to reach the player on the other flank.
- Be aware of the game situation; look for space; sufficient variation between short and long passes.

Positional game ((4v4) + 2)

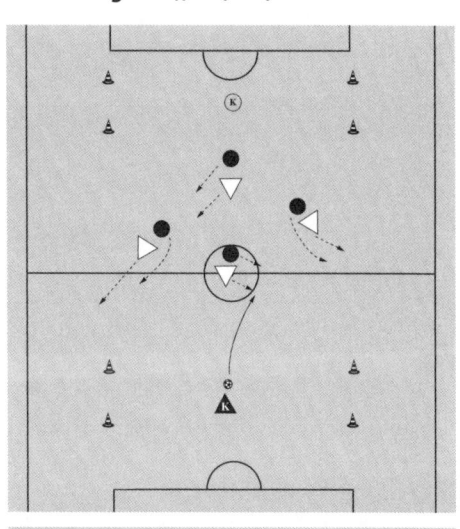

Development objective
Combining the technical skills of build-up play with insight.

Organization
Field: 30 x 15 yards.
Goalkeeper zones: 3 or 4 yards x 15 yards (depending on level of skill).
- Each goalkeeper (K) stands in a zone on the edge of the rectangle.
- We play 4v4.
- The 2 goalkeepers (K) play for the team in possession.
- The defending team can only enter the goalkeeper's zone when he has the ball.
Free play/2-touch play/1-touch play/obligatory 2-touch play/smaller playing area.

Success moment
Ball from goalkeeper to goalkeeper (indirectly = point).

Coaching points
- Formation – see diagram.
- The focus is on the forward pass.
- Everything is done with the aim of passing the ball forward (passing back or passing square = preparation for forward pass)

Book 1   Build-Up Play

6 + goalkeeper v 4

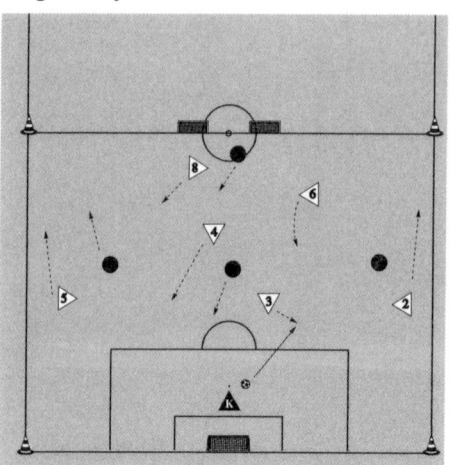

6 + goalkeeper v 5

Development objective
Build-up from the goalkeeper to the defenders and midfielders.

Organization
- We play 6 + goalkeeper v 4.
- Free play.
- The team of 6 scores in the small goals.
- The team of 4 can score in the large goal.
- The positions of the 2 goals can be varied to increase or decrease the level of difficulty for the team of 6.
- When the team of 6 wins a corner, the play restarts with the goalkeeper.

Success moment
A goal has to be scored within a certain time.

Coaching points
- Goalkeeper: Try to play the ball to the most advanced unmarked player.
- Try to find the free player.

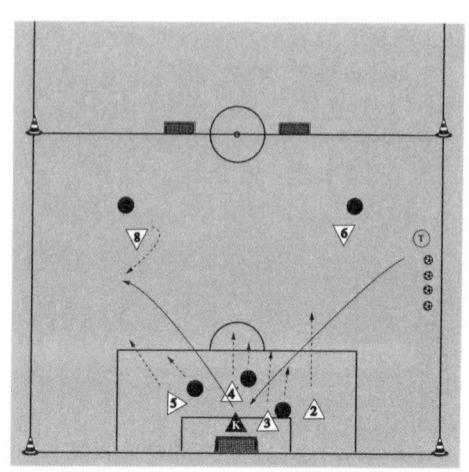

Development objective
Build-up play after a restart play or a cross in front of goal.

Organization
- The coach starts by crossing the ball in front of goal.
- The 3 players in front of the goal try to score in the large goal.
- When the goalkeeper has possession, the players adopt their basic formation and we start with the build-up.
- We choose narrow, high goals.

Success moment
A breakout or goal without any intervention by the attackers counts double.

Coaching points
- Short build-up pass to the defenders who are breaking forward.
- Long build-up pass if one of the wingers is available.

Section 6 - Practice Drills

6 + goalkeeper v 6

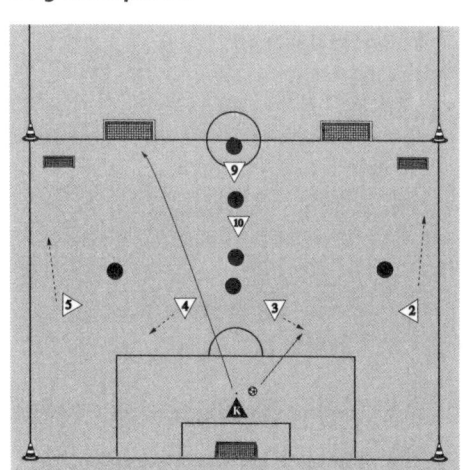

Development objective
Short and long build-up passes by the goalkeeper.

Organization
- The goalkeeper's 6 teammates can score in the 2 small goals.
- The goalkeeper can score by shooting into one of the large empty goals. Pressure must therefore be put on the goalkeeper and someone is always left unmarked.
- The opposing players can score in the large goal defended by the goalkeeper.

Success moment
The winner must decide whether he wants to be or remain a defender.

Coaching points
- Build-up using long or short passes?
- Goalkeeper: Shoot at the empty goal or pass to a player in space?

Book 1 Build-Up Play

Positional play (6v6)

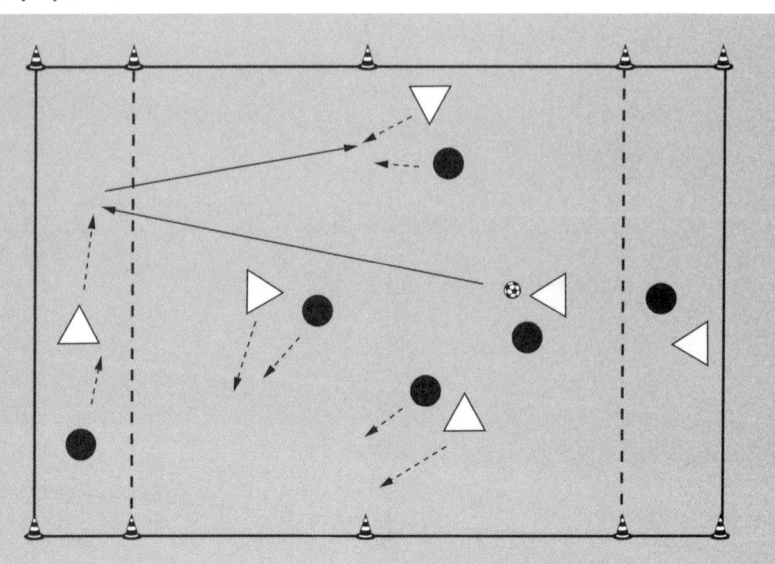

Development objective
Passing the ball forward.

Organization
Size of the field: 30 x 15 yards.
Zones at the ends: 10 x 15 yards (depending on the level of the players).
- One pair of players (circle and triangle) is in each end zone.
- Two teams of 4 players are in the center zone.
- The triangles try to keep possession and to play the ball to their teammates in the 2 end zones (each of these players has a direct opponent).
- All of the players stay in their zones.
- The circles try to win possession and then to keep possession and play the ball to their teammates in the 2 end zones (each of these players has a direct opponent).
- Free play/2-touch play/1-touch play/obligatory 2-touch play/smaller playing area.

Success moment
Build-up from end zone to end zone without losing possession = one point. Who is the first to score 5 points?

Coaching points
- Formation: see diagram.
- The focus is on the forward pass.
- Everything is done with the aim of passing the ball forward (passing back or passing square = preparation for forward pass)
- The forward pass should be played when the defender challenges for the ball.
- Use good positional play to reach the player on the other flank.
- Be aware of the game situation; look for space; sufficient variation between short and long passes.
- Player in the end zone: Try to lose your marker.

Section 6 - Practice Drills

7 + goalkeeper v 6

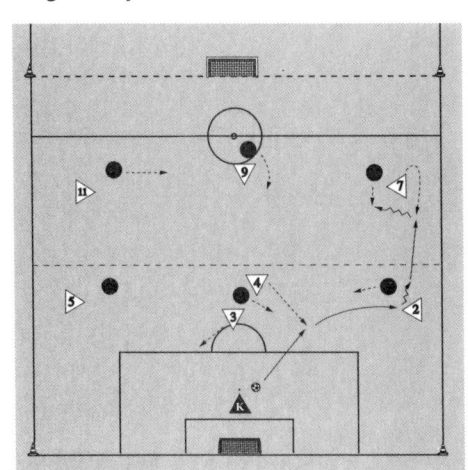

Development objective
Build-up from the goalkeeper to the defenders, and the continuation.

Organization
- We play in 2 zones
- The goalkeeper always starts the build-up with a short pass (4 + goalkeeper v 3).
- The 4 players in the defensive zone try to get the ball to the attackers in the attacking zone.
- The division into zones is then dropped and we play 7 + goalkeeper v 6. The team of 7 can score in the large goal with headers. The team of 6 can score in the large goal defended by the goalkeeper.
- If the 3 players in the build-up zone can win the ball and score, the goal counts double.

Success moment
10 repeats. Who wins?

Coaching points
- Fast ball circulation
- Look for the free man.

Book 1   Build-Up Play

Positional game ((4v4) + 4)

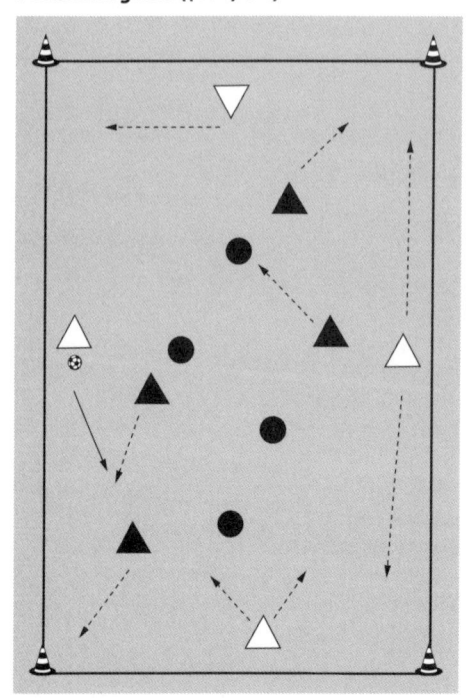

Development objective
The forward pass.

Organization
Size of field: 25 x 25 yards.
- One team of 4 tries to keep possession with the help of the 4 neutral players.
- The other 4 players try to win the ball.
Free play; 2-touch play.
Neutral players: Free; maximum of 2 touches, or one touch only.

Success moment
The coach secretly measures how much time the team of 4 needs to win the ball. The team must then win the ball 3 times within this time (with rest breaks).

Coaching points
- The focus is on the forward pass.
- We try to divide up the space as effectively as possible (for the positions).
- We try to reach the other end of the field.
- Ensure that you are always available.
- Don't always stay at the same level on the flank or in the middle.
- Take up positions at an angle to the player in possession; don't approach the ball head-on; force your opponent to make choices.
- Don't move too fast toward the ball; don't close down your own space.

Section 6 - Practice Drills

Game drill (8v8)

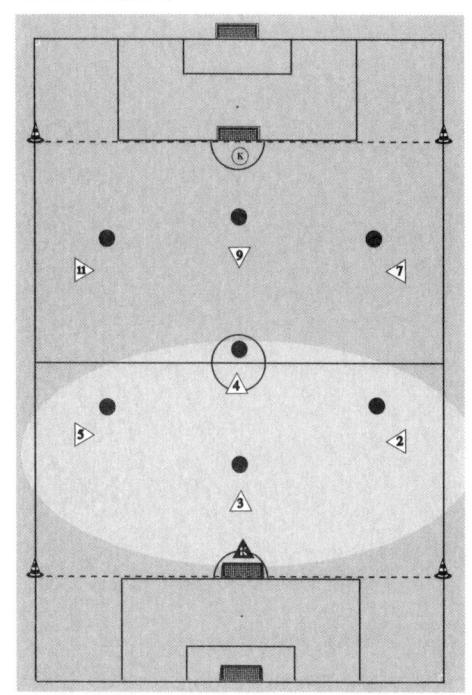

Development objective
Cooperation between defenders and midfielders.

Organization
Task
Aim: To encourage build-up play from the back.
- Each time the ball goes out of play, the play restarts with the goalkeeper.

Success moment
Goals scored after a short or long-passing build-up move started by the goalkeeper, without any intervention by defenders, count double.

Book 1   Build-Up Play

Line training with 3 lines

8v7
8v8
9v6
9v7
9v8
9v9
10v8
10v9
10v10
11v10
11v11   Game drill

Section 6 - Practice Drills

Positional game (8 + goalkeeper v 7)

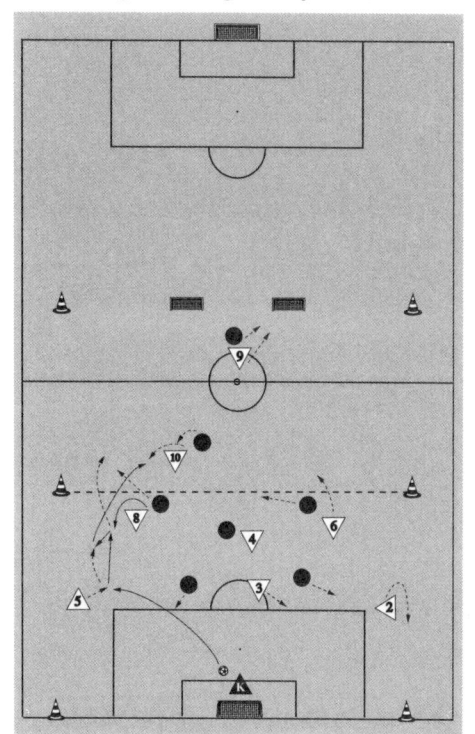

Development objective
Cooperation between defenders and midfielders.

Organization
- We play 6 + goalkeeper v 5 in the build-up zone.
- The team of 6 tries to get the ball to one of the 2 strikers.
- The team of 5 tries to win the ball and score in the large goal.
- When the team of 6 gets the ball to one of the strikers in the attacking zone, the 2 midfielders (6 and 8) and a defender move up in support.
- The 4 attackers can score in one of the small goals.
- The 3 defenders can score by playing the ball to a teammate on the imaginary line.

Success moment
Ten build-up moves from the back – how many goals were scored?

Coaching points
- Be patient.
- Try to find the free man.
- Fast ball circulation.
- Everyone joins in.
- The forward pass is the preferred option.

Book 1 Build-Up Play

Positional game (9 + goalkeeper v 6)

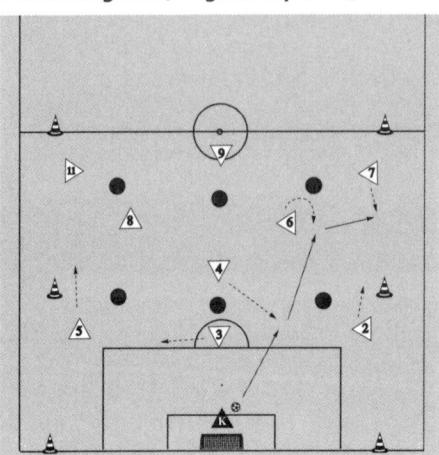

Development objective
Keeping possession during the build-up play.

Organization
- The team of 9 tries to keep possession.
- The team of 6 tries to win the ball and score in the large goal.
- When a goal is scored, the play is restarted by the goalkeeper.
- All of the players play in their own specific positions.

Success moment
The team of 9 can score by circulating the ball 10 times. The team of 6 can score in the large goal.

Coaching points
- Use the space that is created.
- If the ball is circulated too slowly, the team of 6 can exert pressure.

This drill can be made more difficult by limiting the number of ball contacts by certain players or by reducing the size of the field.

Positional game (9 + goalkeeper v 7)

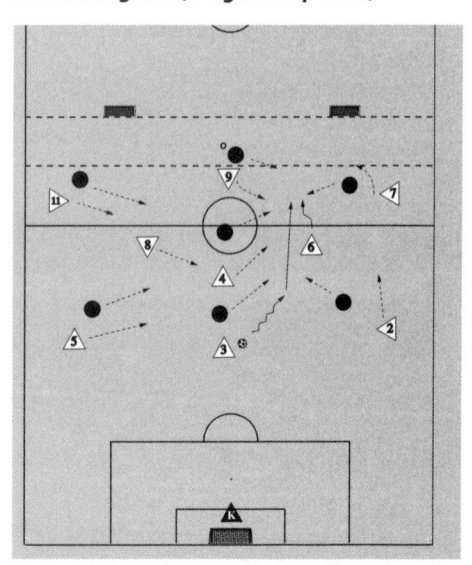

Development objective
Playing a forward pass during the build-up play.

Organization
- The team of 9 can score in one of the 2 small goals beyond the imaginary line.
- After a goal is scored, the team of 7 builds up a move in the opposite direction and tries to score in the large goal.

Success moment
The team of 9 scores within a period of time (= guide period). It then tries to score the next goal faster (if it succeeds, it is awarded a point; if it does not, the team of 7 is awarded a point). If the team of 7 scores a goal, it is awarded a point. Who is first to score 4 points?

Coaching points
- Try to get the ball to the most advanced player.
- Always choose the option that gets the ball furthest forward.
- Stay calm on the ball.
- Look for space.

134

Section 6 - Practice Drills

Positional game (9 + goalkeeper v 8)

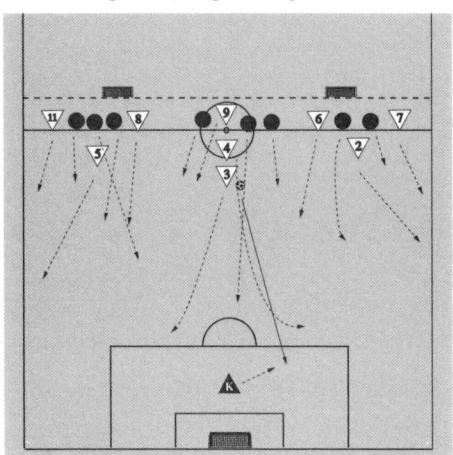

Positional game (9 + goalkeeper v 9)

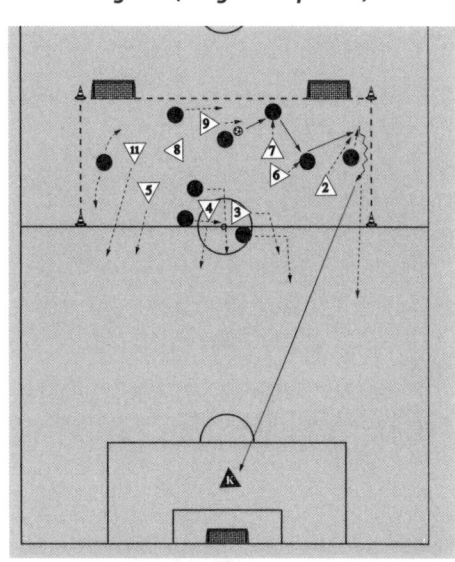

Development objective
Build-up play after a backpass.

Organization
- All of the players start on the center line.
- The central defender starts the drill by playing the ball to the goalkeeper (backpass).
- All the players take up their positions.
- The team of 9 can score in one of the 2 small goals if the ball has crossed the imaginary line.
- The team of 7 scores in the large goal.

Success moment
Who scores first?

Coaching points
- See the basic principles of the backpass.
- Who is the free man?
- Who is the most advanced free man?

The team of 7 players can be given various tasks.
- Pressure the defenders.
- Pressure the midfielders.
- No pressure – play a waiting game.

Development objective
Build-up play after a backpass.

Organization
- We play 9v9 in the zone.
- One team tries to retain possession.
- The players of the other team try to win the ball. If they succeed, they can pass the ball back to their goalkeeper.
- All the players then take up their positions and we play 9 + goalkeeper v 9 over the whole field.
- The goalkeeper's teammates can score in one of the small goals.
- Their opponents can score in the large goal.
- As far as possible, the players play in their own positions.

Success moment
Who scores 5 goals first? If the circles succeed in circulating the ball 6 or 7 or 8 times, they win a point and we start again.

Coaching points
- See the basic principles of the backpass and build-up play.

Book 1   Build-Up Play

10 + goalkeeper v 8

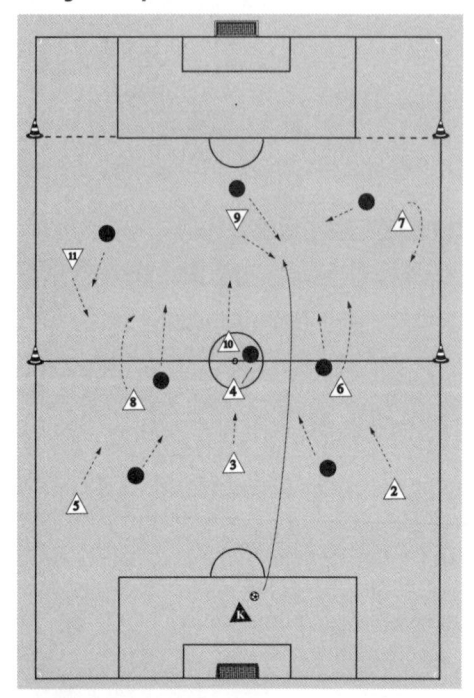

10 + goalkeeper v 9

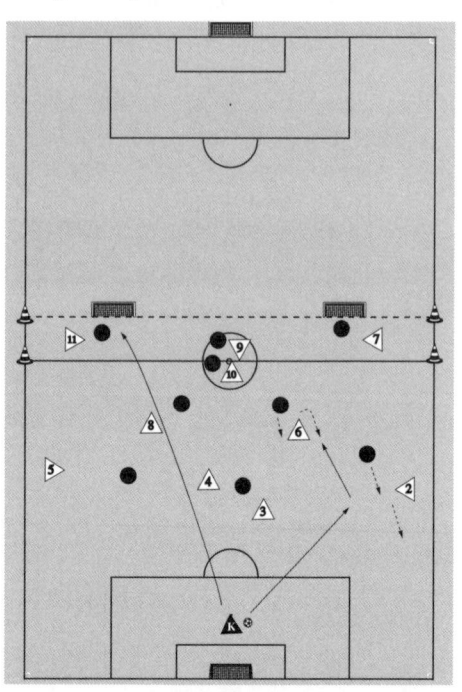

Development objective
Playing the forward pass – cooperation between defenders, midfielders and attackers.

Organization
- This drill is suitable for focusing on build-up play using long passes.
- The team of 10 tries to get the ball to one of the 3 strikers in the attacking zone.
- The other players can then cross the imaginary line and move up in support.
- The team of 10 can score by dribbling the ball over the line.
- The team of 8 can score in the large goal.

Success moment
The team of 8 leads 1-0.

Coaching points
- Don't be tempted to play the forward pass too hastily.
- Be patient
- Circulate the ball quickly.

Development objective
Cooperation between defenders, midfielders and attackers.

Organization
- The goalkeeper can score with a long ball into one of the goals.
- The team of 10 can score in one of the 2 large goals.
- The team of 9 can score in the large goal.
- The imaginary line can be shifted to increase or decrease the level of difficulty.

Success moment
Series of 8 minutes – who wins the first 3 series?

Coaching points
- Forward pass into space (the goal).
- Forward pass to the attackers.
- Forward pass to the midfielders.
- Pass to the defenders.

Section 6 - Practice Drills

10 + goalkeeper v 10

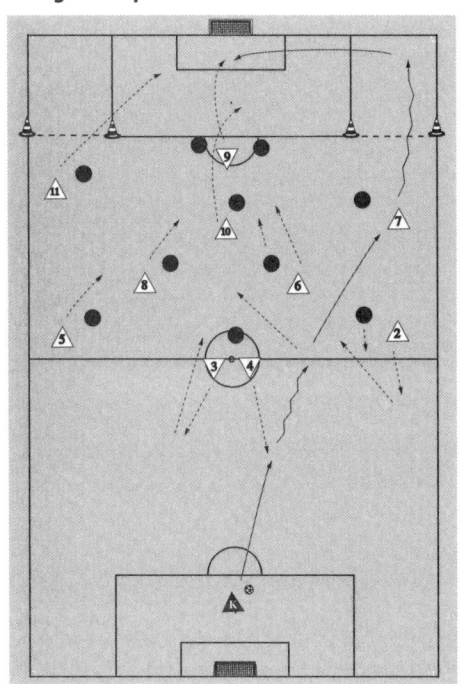

Competitive drill (11v11)

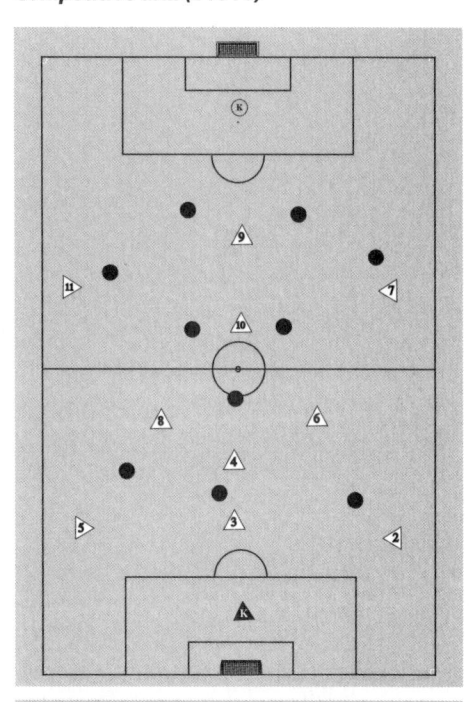

Development objective
Cooperation between defenders, midfielders and attackers.

Organization
- The team with the goalkeeper can score by dribbling the ball between one of the pairs of cones and by heading the ball into the large goal.
- The other team can score in the large goal defended by the goalkeeper.
- All the players must have crossed the center line when a goal is scored.

Success moment
Who is the first to score 5 goals?

Coaching points
- Can we pass directly to the winger or via a number of short passes?

Development objective
The competitive drill is based on a soccer problem.

Organization
Task
Aim: Dealing with the resistance of the opposing team.
- Team A allows the opposing team to build up a move and then exerts pressure when player X (the least secure player in build-up play) has the ball.
- Depending on the situation, team B builds-up its moves as effectively as possible.

Success moment
Goals scored after a move that started with the goalkeeper count double.

Coaching points
- Where is there space?
- Where does the opposing team exert pressure?
- What are the opposing team's strengths?
- Where are the opposing team's weaknesses?

137